TRANSFERRING JUVENILES TO CRIMINAL COURTS

TRANSFERRING JUVENILES TO CRIMINAL COURTS

Trends and Implications for Criminal Justice

DEAN J. CHAMPION and G. LARRY MAYS

Westport, Connecticut
London

Library of Congress Cataloging-in-Publication Data

Champion, Dean J.
　　Transferring juveniles to criminal courts : trends and
implications for criminal justice / Dean J. Champion and G. Larry
Mays.
　　　　p.　　cm.
　　Includes bibliographical references and indexes.
　　ISBN 0-275-93534-5 (alk. paper)
　　　1. Juvenile courts—United States.　2. Criminal courts—United
States.　3. Jurisdiction—United States.　4. Juvenile justice,
Administration of—United States.　　I. Mays, G. Larry.　　II. Title.
KF9794.C48　1991
345.73'081—dc20
[347.30581]　　　　　90-40798

British Library Cataloguing-in-Publication Data is available.

Library of Congress Catalog Card Number: 90–40798
ISBN: 0–275–93534–5

First published in 1991

Praeger Publishers, 88 Post Road West, Westport, CT 06881
An imprint of Greenwood Publishing Group, Inc.

Printed in the United States of America

The paper used in this book complies with the
Permanent Paper Standard issued by the National
Information Standards Organization (Z39.48–1984).

10 9 8 7 6 5 4 3 2

Copyright Acknowledgments

The authors and the publisher are grateful to the following for granting use of their material:

Tables 3.5, 3.6, and 3.7 from Dean Champion, ''Teenage Felons and Waiver Hearings: Some Recent Trends, 1980–1988.'' *Crime and Delinquency* 35, no. 4: pp. 577–85, copyright © 1989 by Sage Publications, Inc. Reprinted by permission of Sage Publications, Inc.

Table 5.1 from Joseph W. Rogers and G. Larry Mays, *Juvenile Delinquency and Juvenile Justice* (Englewood Cliffs, NJ: Prentice-Hall, 1987), pp. 364–65. Copyright © 1987 by Prentice-Hall. Reprinted by permission of Prentice-Hall.

Contents

Figure and Tables

Preface

Transferring Juveniles to Criminal Courts is about a growing and increasingly important phenomenon for both the criminal and juvenile justice systems. During the last several decades numerous reforms have been suggested or implemented throughout the criminal justice process. These reforms have pertained to sentencing procedures, greater emphasis on equating punishments to fit crimes in accordance with "just deserts" and justice, greater inmate access to the courts and the increased sophistication of inmate litigation, experiments with alternative intermediate punishments, and the introduction of an assortment of interventions designed to prevent crime or deter criminals. The perception of a rising tide of crime has been countered with a series of "get tough" policies for offender processing and management. A concomitant of these and other massive reforms throughout the criminal justice system has been a major policy shift regarding the treatment and processing of serious juvenile offenders. Since the mid-1960s juveniles have incurred substantial legal rights almost commensurate with those enjoyed by adults. While in some states a unified court system is still a remote event that may or may not occur in future years, it is significant that juvenile courts have taken on many of the characteristics of criminal courts in processing juveniles charged with various offenses.

Several interesting parallels may be noted. First, criminal courts have been overwhelmed with greater numbers of cases to process, particularly as juvenile courts have become more adversarial in recent years. One reaction from prosecutors and judges has been to prioritize cases according to their seriousness, and reduce the amount of court time allocated, to only the most serious offenses alleged. Plea bargaining and diversion have eased court dockets considerably, and many would-be criminal cases have been redefined as torts and resolved civilly through alternative dispute resolution or some other equivalent measure. Accordingly, juvenile courts have been glutted with cases, and less serious offenders have been redefined, by authorities, as status offenders. Deinstitutionalization of status offenders, or their removal from the jurisdiction of juvenile courts, appears to be one avenue whereby juvenile court dockets have been eased.

Less serious criminal offenders have been granted probation or sentenced to conditional punishments, instead of being incarcerated. Prison and jail overcrowding have contributed significantly to the great increase in adult conditional and intermediate punishments. Juveniles have received similar treatment—as juvenile judges and others have opted for nominal or noncustodial, conditional punishments—including fines, community services, or intensive supervised probation. Like adult incarcerative facilities, juvenile detention facilities in most jurisdictions are currently overcrowded. Authorities must think of innovative ways whereby such juvenile overcrowding problems may be alleviated.

Almost every jurisdiction currently has habitual offender statutes, where those most chronic, repeat offenders or recidivists are potentially liable for sentences of life imprisonment. On the surface at least, this life sentence provision seems a tough penalty for those who are persistent offenders; however, life sentences are imposed on such offenders infrequently. Most habitual offenders do not receive life sentences, since such sentences would cause present serious prison and jail overcrowding to skyrocket.

For certain chronic or persistent juvenile offenders aged fourteen to seventeen, especially the most dangerous and violent juveniles who pose serious public risks, the "get tough" movement has led to greater invocation of transfers or waivers, whereby the jurisdiction over juveniles is transferred to criminal courts. The theory behind such transfers is that criminal courts are in the position of being able to impose more serious penalties on juveniles (such as the death penalty) that would be outside of juvenile court judges' jurisdiction. Again, on the surface such a measure seems consistent with public attitudes that we should be more strict in our handling of juveniles alleged to have committed serious offenses.

However, there is evidence suggesting that our "get tough" measures for criminals and juveniles alike are not having the desired and intended consequences, namely, harsher penalties. It is ironic that as one consequence of the "get tough" movement, in recent years more adults have been subjected to criminal prosecution. Yet, it is also true that in recent years greater proportions of adults have been placed in nonincarcerative intermediate punishment programs, since there is little or no room presently available in prisons to house them. Therefore, our "get tough" strategy has created the optimum conditions for less stringent treatment for adult offenders, as correctional professionals continually seek better ways to manage growing numbers of nonincarcerated offenders.

Additionally, applying the "get tough" system to juveniles does not seem to be targeting the most serious juvenile offenders for transfer to criminal courts. Many chronic juvenile offenders are petty offenders, and often juvenile court judges will transfer them to criminal courts simply to rid themselves of perennial problems. Once transferred to criminal courts, these less serious juvenile offenders blend in with the least serious adult offenders, and they are treated similarly, by being granted probation. In most instances, youthfulness functions as a mitigating circumstance, and many cases against juveniles are not prosecuted. There is simply too much of a backlog of more serious criminal cases, and the likelihood of incarceration for youthful offenders is very remote. Thus, the most serious juvenile offenders are not always the ones who are the targets of transfers.

This book examines the transfer process and describes the types of juveniles who are waived to criminal court jurisdiction. Different jurisdictions have varying standards about how juveniles are defined and at what ages they may be transferred to adult status for possible punishment. Included in this analysis are a description of juvenile courts, the types of juvenile offenders who are processed by these courts, and an examination of the types of outcomes that characterize the majority of transfers.

Chapter 1 discusses the social and legal definitions of delinquency, differences between status and delinquent offenders, and changing patterns of juvenile case processing among jurisdictions. Chapter 2 is an overview of the juvenile justice system. Included in this overview are descriptions of several judicial options, such as nominal, conditional, and detention adjudications. The full range of juvenile punishments is explored, together with an examination of public policy and the theme of deterring juvenile offenders.

Chapter 3 describes transfers, also known as certifications or waivers in different jurisdictions. The goals and functions of transfers are described. Several different types of transfers are investigated, together with a preliminary assessment of which juveniles are transferred most frequently and the general outcomes of these transfers. Chapter 4 further explores the various implications of transfers for juvenile offenders. Once juvenile offenders are transferred to criminal court, jury trials are available as a matter of right for those charged with crimes justifying incarceration for six months or more. Furthermore, incarceration for lengthy periods as well as the death penalty are likely options for transferred youthful offenders, if convicted. Again, public policy is examined as it relates to the espoused goals of the "get tough" policy that is prevalent throughout the juvenile justice system.

Chapter 5 describes the criminal court and some of the varied functions served by these courts. As larger numbers of juveniles are waived to criminal court jurisdiction annually, both prosecutors and judges must evaluate their methods of prosecuting and judging these youthful offenders contrasted with their adult counterparts. Juvenile rights affect the process of jurisdictional transfers. Since the mid-1960s, juveniles have incurred many constitutional rights that were formerly denied them (or simply ignored) under the doctrine of *parens patriae*. Juveniles and their defense attorneys must carefully examine the options; in some instances being transferred to criminal courts may not be entirely negative for affected juveniles. Finally, Chapter 6 summarizes several important trends relating to juvenile transfers. Included here are male and female juvenile comparisons, the issue of selective certification, and certain implications for prison and jail overcrowding, and the subsequent emergence of a unified court system.

CHAPTER 1

Juvenile Delinquents, Status Offenders, and Public Policy: An Introduction

During the last several decades, a gradual disenchantment with the criminal justice system has occurred. Seemingly, citizens have acquired a strong degree of cynicism about law enforcement, the courts, and corrections, and their respective abilities to process, punish, and manage offenders. The U.S. Supreme Court has obligated law enforcement officers to adhere to more rigid standards in effecting arrests of suspected criminals, as well as in their procedures for seizing inculpatory evidence against these suspects. Over 90 percent of all criminal convictions are presently secured against defendants through plea bargaining in lieu of trial, and the use of probation as a correctional alternative is as high as 70 percent in many jurisdictions. Furthermore, most offenders who are incarcerated serve only a fraction of their sentences and are conditionally released on parole. The public has sensed a growing laxity toward offenders, and this laxity seems pervasive throughout the entire criminal justice system.

One reaction to this real or imaginary laxity has been the emergence of the "get tough" movement, evidenced by modifications of sentences imposed on adults convicted of serious crimes. These sentences include longer prison terms, heavier fines and other monetary penalties, together with other punitive measures. There has been a noticeable spillover effect of this "get tough" movement into the juvenile justice system as well. The causes célèbres such as the terrorizing of Bernard Goetz on a subway, by teenagers, and the rape of a woman jogger in New York City's Central Park by a gang of vicious youths who believed they had left her for dead, have done little to promote a lenient attitude among the public toward youthful offenders and how they are punished.

Reported trends of increasing violent crime among adolescents have furthered the fears of legislators and their constituencies (Strasburg 1984). For instance, between 1960 and 1975, juvenile arrests grew by nearly 300 percent, more than twice the violent crime arrest rate for adults. Also focusing public attention on the influx of juveniles into violent crime circles was the fact that in 1975, juveniles aged seven to seventeen accounted for 43 percent of the FBI's seven major index offenses (e.g., aggravated assault, robbery, homicide, forcible rape, burglary, larceny, and vehicular theft), although they comprised only 20 percent of the nation's population that same year (Strasburg 1984). Especially noticeable was the rise of gang-related juvenile offenses, particularly in areas such as New York, Chicago, and Los Angeles (Maxon et al. 1986). Greater access to automobiles, firearms, and drugs has no doubt correlated highly with increased juvenile violence (Cornell et al. 1987; Hartstone and Hansen 1984; Heuser 1985; Kriesman and Siden 1982; Youth Policy and Law Center, Inc. 1984).

Despite subsequent trends and estimates of juvenile offense patterns and inconsistent and inconclusive statistics, substantial juvenile court reform was provoked, has continued into the 1990s, and shows few, if any, signs of abating (Agopian 1989; Hartstone et al. 1986). Although "get tough" policies toward juveniles have been supported by most jurisdictions, greater detention and incarceration of youths has not proven to be a panacea for rehabilitating them or reducing their recidivism (Schwartz 1989). Largely because of inconsistencies in study findings and unremarkable outcomes of detention programs as therapeutic juvenile interventions, many states are currently reexamining their detention provisions for minors and reducing their reliance on detention as punishment (Schwartz 1989).

Among the explanatory factors that have contributed to these statistical inconsistencies and peculiar juvenile offense trends—especially during the 1980s—has been (1) a general disenchantment with conventional juvenile treatments such as diversion, probation, short-term detention and parole (Curran 1988; Dobbert 1987; Gelber 1988); (2) apparent psychological concomitants of juvenile violence that lie beyond the parameters of conventional treatment methods (Cornell et al. 1987; Goldstein and Glick 1987; Plutichik 1983); and (3) diverse classificatory and reporting methods and changing laws among jurisdictions as consistent means of charting errant juveniles (Blackmore et al. 1988; Farnworth et al. 1988; Krisberg 1988; McCarthy 1989).

Compared with adult courts, juvenile courts are significantly limited in the types of sanctions they may impose for even the most violent juvenile offenders. Criminal courts in a majority of U.S. jurisdictions may impose the death penalty on adult offenders convicted of capital crimes. No U.S. juvenile court, however, has this type of powerful jurisdiction and sanctioning option. Even detention sanctions that may be applied by juvenile judges have certain structural limitations; once juveniles reach the age of majority, eighteen in some states and twenty-one in others, they are no longer within the purview of juvenile courts and most often exit the system. They also enjoy the privilege of clean records as adults. Their juvenile records are not necessarily absolved, but for all practical purposes they begin their adulthood technically without a criminal past.

When records of juvenile judges are examined to determine the nature and types of punishments processed juvenile offenders receive if they are subsequently adjudicated as delinquent, these records reflect a consistent pattern of leniency. This leniency may stem from judicial reluctance to contribute to labeling juvenile offenders as delinquent. However, it is often traced to extraneous factors such as juvenile detention facility overcrowding, excessive juvenile probation officer caseloads, and the lack of adequate juvenile monitoring programs and methods to keep track of burgeoning numbers of youthful offenders (Fox and Viegas 1987; Kueneman et al. 1985). Thus, it may be a simple matter of being unable to afford the imposition of costly punishments whenever they are warranted. The exigencies of the situation tie the judges' hands, and they are left to deal "leniently" with juveniles, even violent ones.

One option that may be exercised by juvenile courts is transferring, waiving, or certifying juveniles to the jurisdiction of adult criminal courts. Transfers, waivers, or certifications are deliberate jurisdictional shifts whereby juvenile courts pass certain juvenile offenders along to be processed as adults. As we will see, there are different ways such transfers or waivers may proceed. For the time being, it is sufficient to understand that the concept of a waiver or transfer, as well as its intent, is to allow other courts to impose more severe punishments than may be contemplated or permitted by statute within juvenile court jurisdiction (Sagatun et al. 1985). Thus, the groundwork is established, theoretically and ideally, of course, for meting out more "just" punishments to certain juveniles than could be imposed by juvenile judges. If juvenile courts cannot impose sufficiently harsh punishments on juveniles, then juveniles should be made accountable and amenable to more severe punishments at the hands of criminal court judges.

This book is about the juvenile transfer or waiver process. Who gets waived to criminal courts? What happens to waived or transferred youths once they are within adult court jurisdiction? Is there unanimity throughout the public sector, supporting the use of transfers as a means of accomplishing this phase of the "get tough" movement's attack on serious juvenile offenders? Experts disagree on the correct answers to each of these questions. While results vary among jurisdictions, it is not always the case that the most dangerous, violent, or serious juvenile offenders are the subject of waiver or transfer motions (August 1984; Feld 1984a; New Jersey Division of Criminal Justice 1985; Nimick et al. 1986). Once youths have been placed within criminal court jurisdiction, they do not always receive maximum punishments or the harshest penalties. In fact, many youths receive no punishment when treated as adults (Bortner 1986; Decker 1984; Reed 1983; Schack and Nessen 1984). Finally, not everyone agrees that juvenile waivers are meritorious and should be used on a large scale (August 1981; Feld 1987b, 1989; Harris and Graff 1988; Thomas and Bilchik 1985).

This chapter distinguishes between the social and legal definitions of delinquency. There are substantial jurisdictional differences that influence these definitions. Various types of youthful offenders are described. Juvenile courts deal with a broad range of youths, often encompassing unmanageable or unruly children, curfew violators, runaways and truants, or alleged murderers, rapists, and robbers at the other end of the offense spectrum. Attention will be given to several trends during the past few decades to remove some of the less serious juveniles from court settings to more treatment-oriented, community-based settings. While some of these options have sought to minimize the problems associated with juvenile processing and treatment, at times the problems have been exacerbated.

Juvenile violence will be examined, as well as the interplay between the juvenile courts and various community agencies, as each attempts to help, through different types of intervention strategies. Public policy relating to juveniles will be assessed, especially as it has functioned to influence the development or abandonment of various laws and programs designed to process youthful offenders.

SOCIAL AND LEGAL DEFINITIONS OF DELINQUENCY

There are many social and legal definitions of delinquency. Each state has devised a formal, legal definition of delinquency, and considerable variation exists among states about how delinquency is conceptualized. This diversity is evident in gender and age criteria as well as in specific behavior or acts that fall within the delinquency rubric. Social definitions of delinquency depend largely on those who engage in defining the behavior of others. Obviously, there are both time and place dimensions associated with these highly subjective impressions about who is or is not delinquent. Interpretations made by adults, of deviant conduct observed among youths, are often equated with delinquency.

Our present social and legal definitions of delinquency have been influenced greatly by early English common law, especially during the medieval period. In medieval times, matters relating to children or youthful adults were regulated under the doctrine of *parens patriae*. This doctrine indicated that the king of England (or his agents, representatives or chancellors) was figuratively the father of the country and, as such, he assumed almost absolute responsibility for all juvenile affairs (Black 1979:385). Thus, the king's chancellors adjudicated all matters involving youths. These decisions were independent of the jurisdiction of English criminal courts.

Those subject to the chancellors' discretion during medieval times were often referred to as minors, children, or infants, although sometimes they were defined as "not having reached the age of majority" (Black 1979:899). For all practical purposes, the age of majority was considered to be eighteen years. Also, under English common law, children under age seven were presumed incapable of formulating criminal intent, regardless of the seriousness of their behavior. As such, they were not subject to penalties for misbehavior other than family-administered corporal punishments (e.g., spanking). Typical behavior of infants that brought them within the chancellors' purview included incorrigibility, unmanageability, running away, loitering, trespassing, poaching, and most minor mischievous, not necessarily criminal, conduct.

During the formative years of the United States, English common law had a strong influence on how juveniles were defined and processed. During the Industrial Revolution, when thousands of families migrated to large cities to obtain work, many young children were often left unsupervised for long periods during both day and night. Although compulsory education for youths existed in most major jurisdictions, such compulsion was difficult to enforce. Thus, unruly and unsupervised youths running rampant on city streets was commonplace. Religious and philanthropic interests, during the early 1800s, established houses of refuge to provide shelter, food, and clothing for errant youths as well as some degree of adult supervision. The first public reformatory in the United States was established in 1825. Known as the New York House of Refuge, and widely imitated in subsequent years in other cities, this reformatory was of questionable value as a rehabilitative medium (Cahalan 1986; Rogers and Mays 1987:426).

The first juvenile court was established in Illinois in 1899. That same year, the Colorado legislature passed the Compulsory School Act which authorized formal sanctions to punish youthful truants. During the next ten years, twenty other states established juvenile courts, and by 1945, all states had formal juvenile court apparatuses in place (Cahalan 1986).[1] Concomitant with these developments, both public and private programs and services for juveniles were created and operated with varying degrees of success throughout different communities. Divisions of family services, social welfare agencies, and human services departments have continued to function in tandem with juvenile courts over the years, in attempting to meet various needs of referred juveniles.

A simple legal definition of delinquency is any act committed by someone of not more than a specified age (eighteen in most jurisdictions) that would otherwise be considered a felony or misdemeanor if committed by an adult. This definition is found in one form or another in all state statutes that define delinquent conduct. In federal courts juvenile delinquents are those who have violated a criminal law of the United States prior to their eighteenth birthday (18 U.S.C. Sec. 5031, 1990).[2] However, other behaviors besides criminal ones frequently are included under the heading of delinquency, including children in need of supervision, unmanageable or unruly children, runaways, truants, and sometimes those who are neglected and dependent.

Considerable discretion exists among law enforcement officers and others about how they each choose to label certain types of juvenile behavior. At any given stage of the justice process (see Chapter 2), various juveniles may be referred to community agencies for less formal processing. Police officers may issue warnings to certain youths rather than take them into custody for investigation and processing. In many jurisdictions, legislators have attempted to remove certain types of juveniles from formal juvenile court processing (see "The Deinstitutionalization of Status Offenses" later in this chapter for an extended discussion of this process). If we argue that running away from home or having excessive unexcused school absences are considerably less serious than murder, rape, or robbery, we might recommend supervision of the former class of youths by a community service agency, whereas incarceration in a juvenile correctional facility might be in order for the latter class of offenders. This would seem "just" or fair to many interested citizens.

Unfortunately, these obvious distinctions and dispositions do not always have their intended, "justice-oriented" consequences. For example, a truant youth may be diverted from juvenile court and placed, under orders from a family court, in a group or foster home, or in some community treatment facility for periodic therapy and counseling. However, failure to conform to the rules of group or foster homes or to attend therapy treatment or counseling sessions places the juvenile in violation of a valid court order. This violation is a crime and the youth will be arrested and eventually redefined by the court as delinquent.[3] Therefore, the system often has a built-in escalation factor that makes mountains out of molehills. If some youths targeted for special community treatment have been chronically unmanageable, incorrigible, or truant, it is unlikely that any court order will magically induce instant compliance with program rules and regulations. In a sense, this is structured failure, and it seems pervasive in most jurisdictions.

The legal definition of delinquency always specifies an upper age range, variable among state and federal jurisdictions, although there is considerable ambiguity regarding the minimum age where juvenile courts may exercise jurisdiction. Regarding transfers, for instance, some states (e.g., Alaska, Maine, Wyoming) leave unspecified the minimum age for certifying youths as adults. Rather, they rely heavily upon offense seriousness in making their transfer or waiver decisions. Ages sixteen to seventeen, for transfer consideration, are most prevalent throughout U.S. jurisdictions. (Chapter 3 discusses the transfer process in considerable detail.)

TYPES OF OFFENDERS

Juveniles who are subject to the jurisdiction of juvenile courts may be "typed" in several ways. Following the *Uniform Crime Reports* offense classifications published annually by the FBI, arrests of suspects are reported according to Part 1 and Part 2 offenses. Part 1 offenses consist of eight "index crimes," further distinguished according to "violent" and "property" offenses. Violent crimes include murder, forcible rape, robbery, and aggravated assault. Property crimes include burglary, larceny-theft, motor vehicle theft, and arson. Part 2 offenses include, but are not limited to, embezzlement, forgery, vandalism, curfew and loitering law violations, drunkenness, disorderly conduct, prostitution and commercialized vice, vagrancy, suspicion, drug abuse violations, stolen property, carrying weapons, driving under the influence, and liquor law violations. While several of the Part 2 offenses are similar in seriousness to several of the index offenses, some of the Part 2 categories contain a disproportionately large number of youths under age eighteen, contrasted with other age categories. Each year, those under age eighteen make up varying proportions of all Part 1 and Part 2 offenses categories.

Criminal justice and criminology professionals describe juvenile offenders using several of the above designations, although widespread agreement about how juveniles should best be classified is nonexistent. For example, Rubin (1985a) describes "three main types of cases" that come before juvenile court judges: delinquency, status offenses, and child neglect and abuse. Some studies target specific offender groupings such as "sex offenders" or "drug- or alcohol-dependent" for intensive investigation (Calhoun and Pickerill 1988; Fagan 1988; Hingson et al. 1989; Lombardo and DiGiorgio-Miller 1988; Steen and Monnette 1989). Yet other researchers describe juvenile offenders in terms of committing crimes against the person, major property crime, minor property crime, crimes against the public order, and "other" (Conti et al. 1984).

Probably the most common classifications of juvenile offenders, for research purposes, include *juvenile delinquents* (divided according to violent and property crime designations, and relying heavily on the legal definition of delinquency as any act committed by anyone under a specified age that would be a crime if committed by an adult), and *status offenders* (typically includes truants, runaways, curfew violators, and unruly or otherwise incorrigible children).

Juvenile Delinquents

With certain exceptions of *mala in se* offenses, including murder, rape, aggravated assault, and armed robbery, the seriousness we attach to a juvenile's misconduct is relative. We know, for example, that public perceptions of a rise in juvenile violence has triggered numerous reforms throughout the juvenile justice system, particularly reforms pertaining to the nature and degree of punishment. The violent-nonviolent offense distinction is used by various government agencies to chart juvenile delinquency adjudication, disposition, and detention decisions (American Institutes for Research 1988; Speirs 1989).

Violent offenses typically include criminal homicide, violent sex offenses, robbery, and aggravated assault; while nonviolent offenses consist of "simple" assault, other personal offenses, burglary, theft, other property offenses, drug law violations, and public order offenses (American Institutes for Research 1988). However, even official, government-sponsored projects are clouded with a degree of definitional ambiguity and subjectivity in selecting juvenile clients for treatment. For instance, the Office of Juvenile Justice and Delinquency Prevention (OJJDP) established the Habitual Serious and Violent Juvenile Offender Program (HSVJOP) in mid-1984. "Experienced" prosecutors were relied upon, in part, to furnish this program with qualified juveniles through "selective prosecution." However, an admission by the OJJDP underscores the ambiguity about which juveniles qualify:

The official selection criteria used by this project target youth who are charged with one of the offenses listed in OJJDP's original program announcement—robbery, burglary, rape, aggravated assault, homicide—or another crime against the person. Ordinarily, targeted youth must have a record of at least one prior adjudication for a serious offense. The project will make some exceptions—rejecting a youth who meets the criteria but does not seem "serious" enough, or accepting one who is "borderline" (American Institutes for Research 1988:5).

Interestingly, burglary was included in the OJJDP's original program announcement, although burglary is considered nonviolent and not particularly serious compared with murder and rape. Also, it is not necessarily the case that all nonviolent offenses are also nonserious ones. If we consider "dangerousness" in our evaluation of the seriousness of offenses, drug law violations, driving while intoxicated, and simple assault may be classified as nonviolent but dangerous. With the increased likelihood of AIDS transmission, through greater drug use and unsterilized needles and other drug paraphernalia, many drug offenses may be equated with murder, as deadly viruses are deliberately transmitted to others. Indeed, murder charges have been filed against persons who have knowingly transmitted the AIDS virus either through drug abuse or sexual contact. By the same token, driving while intoxicated may lead to vehicular homicide, and simple assault may cause disabling physical problems for those assaulted.

Since the HSVJOP focuses upon habitual or "chronic" offenders as well as violent and serious ones, it does not necessarily follow that all habitual offenders are violent or serious. Chronicity may include juveniles who have had numerous prior adjudications for burglary, a traditionally nonviolent offense. Again, a strong element of subjectivity is prevalent among different jurisdictions regarding definitions of offense seriousness and violence. The highly decentralized nature of prosecutorial decision making and juvenile referrals among jurisdictions may produce "bad selections of youth who weren't really serious offenders," even where objective selection criteria were operative (American Institutes for Research 1988:9).

For our purposes, juvenile delinquents will be regarded as those persons under a designated age (according to specific jurisdictional criteria) who have been adjudicated (found guilty) by a juvenile or other court, of one or more acts that would have been crimes if committed by adults.

Status Offenders

Status offenses encompass any acts committed by juveniles that would *not* be considered acts if committed by adults. If a senior citizen enrolls in an evening class at a university, for example, and decides not to attend class for several periods, the lack of attendance does not constitute a criminal act. However, if juveniles enrolled in elementary or high schools elect not to attend classes without valid excuses, these are offenses applicable only to juveniles. Typical status offenders include runaways, truants, curfew violators, "wayward children," violators of liquor laws, and unmanageable or incorrigible youths.

Investigators have examined status offender profiles over the years to ascertain whether these individuals "escalate" to more serious offenses that might include criminal behavior. Although research findings have been inconsistent and sketchy about such profiles (Benda 1987; Datesman and Aickin 1985; Rankin and Wells 1985; Rojek and Erickson 1982), certain status offenders, particularly those with alcohol or drug dependencies, seem to constitute a greater "at risk" aggregate compared with those youths without such problems or dependencies (Speck et al. 1988). Recidivist runaways, for instance, stand a greater chance of becoming psychotic or delinquent, compared with "first-timer" runaways (Speck et al. 1988). It has also been found that truants, and curfew and liquor law violators seem more likely to commit more serious offenses in subsequent years, compared with "unmanageables" and runaways (Shelden et al. 1989).

Prior to the 1970s, both alleged status offenders and delinquents appeared in the same juvenile courts to face adjudication and punishment. However, an emerging belief was that greater formal contact

with the juvenile justice system might only succeed in labeling processed youths with the unfavorable "delinquent" connotation. Subsequently labeled as "delinquent" by the formal system, youths might
"act out" the implications of the delinquent label and commit more
serious offenses. Regardless of the merits of this labeling argument,
a divestiture movement occurred in many states, where juvenile
courts were disenfranchised of their jurisdiction over status offenders
(Schneider 1984a). In effect, a movement occurred to remove certain
types of juvenile offenders from the jurisdiction of juvenile courts.
This movement has been popularly known as the "deinstitutionalization of status offenses," or DSO.

THE DEINSTITUTIONALIZATION OF STATUS OFFENSES (DSO)

The deinstitutionalization of status offenses means removing certain types of juvenile offenders from the direct jurisdiction of juvenile
courts (Colley and Culbertson 1988). Status offenses include such
non-crimes as curfew violations, truancy, running away from home,
and being unruly or incorrigible. As we have seen, there are convincing qualitative arguments for stating that some juvenile offenders
commit more serious acts than others (U.S. Senate Judiciary Committee 1984). Thus, subjecting all types of juvenile offenders to the
jurisdiction of juvenile courts, regardless of the seriousness of their
offenses, is considered by many experts to be "overkill" for those
juveniles who do not actually commit crimes (Rankin and Wells
1985).

Especially targeted for deinstitutionalization or divestiture are offenses such as those listed previously (e.g., unruly behavior, curfew
violations), offenses that become "offenses" by virtue of the "status"
of being a juvenile or being within a certain age range when the
offenses are committed (Schneider 1984a). Removing certain offenses from the jurisdiction of juvenile courts and diverting specific
cases to community agencies and organizations, including human
services or social welfare institutions, places deinstitutionalized juveniles in the position of possibly escaping the stigma associated
with the juvenile delinquent label, although professionals disagree
about the true implications of juvenile justice processing in contributing to such unfavorable labeling (Anderson and Schoen 1985).

Many professionals maintain that contemporary juvenile courts manifest many of the criminal courts' characteristics, and that certain juvenile justice reforms have resulted, in part, in the further criminalization of juvenile courts (Feld 1984, 1989). Arguably, these criminalization enhancements have adverse implications for processed juvenile offenders (Binder and Geis 1984; National College of Juvenile and Family Law 1989; Sametz 1984).

Diverting youths from juvenile courts through deinstitutionalization is seen by many of its proponents as decreasing a juvenile's likelihood or propensity to commit more serious crimes, compared with juvenile court adjudications and processing of these same youths as delinquent on noncriminal charges. For example, some research suggests that warnings, dismissals, unofficial probation, or agency referrals of first-time status offenders to community agencies, compared with formal juvenile court detention hearings, drastically reduce recidivism among these offenders (Stewart et al. 1986). This research also discloses similarly favorable results of such alternatives-to-detention programs for those youths whose arrest-offenses were criminal. Other reports indicate that the custodial confinement of status offenders hardens them and increases their likelihood of reoffending (U.S. Senate Judiciary Committee 1984).

Many opponents of deinstitutionalization of status offenses believe that the comparatively light treatment and/or punishment extended status offenders does a gross disservice to these offenders and society, in the long run (Springer 1987). Youths who are adjudicated by juvenile courts on their first contacts, compared with those who are referred to community agencies for treatment, or simply "warned" and returned to parental custody, exhibit less recidivism (Brown et al. 1987). Also, adjudicated juveniles receiving special probation conditions (e.g., restitution orders, community service) have been found to recidivate less than those adjudicated juveniles who receive no special probationary conditions (Nagoshi 1986). However, in another comparison, of youths who were arrested and adjudicated by the juvenile justice system and a sample of youths who had committed felonious acts but had not been caught—those offenders who were subsequently adjudicated became more seriously delinquent afterward—although recidivism differences between the two groups were not substantial (Miller and Gold 1984). Clearly, there are several competing and contrasting juvenile court philosophies (e.g., rationalist and humanitarian) regarding the way "less serious" youths should be managed (Krisberg 1988). Also, not all juvenile courts and justice agencies are equipped equally, with the necessary range of resources, to deal effectively with diverse types of youthful offenders (Krisberg 1988).

It is perhaps misleading to lump all status offenders into a single category, despite the prevailing belief that status offenders have low rates of recidivism (Benda 1987). For instance, evidence suggests that significant differences exist between status offenders who are runaways or otherwise unmanageable and those who are truant, violate curfew, and engage in liquor law violations (Shelden et al. 1989). Based on a longitudinal investigation of 863 youths referred to the Clarke County Juvenile Court in Las Vegas, Nevada, researchers found that truants and curfew violators were much more likely to escalate to more serious crimes in their reoffending behavior than runaways were (Shelden et al. 1989). However, Datesman and Aickin (1985) found no evidence to support the idea that offense escalation occurs among those status offenders who recidivate. Examinations of different types of juveniles in different jurisdictions may explain away some of these contrary findings, however.

Also, runaways themselves do not necessarily constitute a homogeneous group of status offenders (Kufeldt and Perry 1989). A Canadian study of nearly 1,000 juveniles yielded a runaway typology of (1) *throwaways* or homeless; (2) *runaways* exiled from fractured or broken homes, including disenfranchised youths from disadvantaged families; (3) *runners*, whose runaway behavior is of short duration and seasonal; and (4) *runarounds*, who are regarded as temporary escapists seeking adventure and avoidance of boredom (Kufeldt and Perry 1989). Additional research indicates that certain types of runaways are "at risk" to a greater degree than others. While a majority of runaways go only a short distance from their homes and return relatively quickly, others leave for longer periods, to escape troubled families. In turn, they are exposed to life on the streets—replete with violence, drugs, illicit sex, and other problems—including the obvious likelihood of arrest by police (Garbarino et al. 1986).

Another argument challenging the effectiveness and long-term benefits for youths of the deinstitutionalization of status offenses is that "net-widening" is an unintended, adverse consequence of deinstitutionalization (Schneider 1984a). Net-widening occurs whenever certain youths are brought into the juvenile justice system formally, by law enforcement officers, and when the offenses alleged are non-serious ones and could otherwise be overlooked by police.

Washington State enacted a divestiture law, in 1978, that effectively removed status offenses from juvenile court jurisdiction. Thus, incidents such as running away, curfew violation, or truancy were no longer grounds for court referrals, detention, or other types of formal juvenile court sanction (Schneider 1984a). Such divestiture laws removed substantial discretionary powers from police whenever officers encountered alleged status offenders. The intent of this divestiture law was to reduce the numbers of juvenile court petitions filed, to reduce juvenile court workloads, and to manage status offenders outside of the criminalizing atmosphere of juvenile courtrooms, through diversion to community-based agencies and treatment services. However, cities such as Seattle and Yakima reflected great increases in delinquency activity between 1978 and 1980. Significantly more youths were arrested for delinquent acts after the enactment of the divestiture law than before it had been passed. Juvenile court dockets nearly doubled after divestiture (Schneider 1984a).

It would be premature and inaccurate to say that delinquency in Washington doubled between 1978 and 1980. Rather, police officers themselves contributed greatly to inflation of these delinquency figures. It was found, for example, that police officers were relabeling certain behavior as delinquency, in the postdivestiture period, when those same acts would have been mere status offenses in the predivestiture period (Schneider 1984a). Police officers who were interviewed disclosed some antagonism over the fact that the divestiture law robbed them of some of their discretionary power over juveniles. Juvenile judges, seemingly sensing the same loss of discretionary power through divestiture, generally reacted by dealing more harshly with those youths having previous records of status offenses, contrary to the spirit, intent, and letter of Washington law (Schneider 1984a). Both police officers and judges, therefore, objected to the loss of discretionary power relative to status offenders; thus, the very juveniles the divestiture law was designed to protect became prime targets of opportunity, through relabeling by police officers and judges.

Interestingly, the net-widening argument is not in any way, shape, or form a true criticism of the merits of deinstitutionalization. Rather, it draws our attention away from the intended benefits of deinstitutionalization, whether those benefits are avoidance of delinquent labeling, reductions in juvenile court caseloads, or reductions of juvenile detention populations. Net-widening is one adverse consequence of deinstitutionalization, largely because of questionable threats to police and judicial egos and the amount of power they conceivably wield. In principle, deinstitutionalization separates juvenile offenders according to offense seriousness: a laudable goal. In practice, however, diverse elements of the criminal and juvenile justice systems undermine deinstitutionalization's positive benefits, because of nonrational and purely personal reasons.

Furthermore, the success of deinstitutionalization, or lack of it, in removing certain types of youths from the juvenile justice system and effectively decreasing detention rates, prompts some researchers to consider throwing the baby out with the bath water. Indeed, Logan and Rausch (1985), among others, consider deinstitutionalization of status offenses as pointless, relying heavily on the logistics affected by this phenomenon. A deinstitutionalization of status offenses (DSO) program in Connecticut was investigated during the period 1975–1977. According to Logan and Rausch (1985), the gross detention rate was relatively unaffected by DSO during this time interval. However, they conceded that DSO did result in removing or diverting status offenders from Connecticut's primary secure facility for juveniles at Long Lane (Logan and Rausch 1985). Unfortunately, certain questions about DSO remained unanswered. Did affected juveniles, particularly those removed from the state's detention facility, exhibit any significant change in self-concept or self-perception as delinquents? Were significant differences observed in recidivism rates of status offenders diverted to noninstitutional facilities? Answers to these types of questions are crucial if we are to appreciate fully the long-term consequences of DSO.

If deinstitutionalization of status offenses effectively removes less serious juvenile offenders from the juvenile justice system as intended, then those who are subsequently processed by the system may, in turn, be differentiated according to a higher standard of offense seriousness. Theoretically, this will make it easier for judges and others to initiate waivers or certifications, as only the most serious offenders will be targeted for criminal court jurisdiction. But as we have seen, it is possible for some persistent, or chronic, status offenders to be remanded to criminal court jurisdiction: largely because of their persistence or chronicity and because of their "criminal" noncompliance with court-ordered participation in non-institutional, community-based programs designed to prevent them from acquiring the delinquent label.

Juvenile Violence and Violence Trends

For both juveniles and adults, violent offenses traditionally include homicide, rape, robbery, and aggravated assault (Rogers and Mays 1987:545). Describing juvenile violence and violence trends is inherently flawed by the many limitations and weaknesses of our available information sources and outlets, such as the *Uniform Crime Reports, National Crime Survey,* and assorted reports on victimization (Menard 1987: U.S. Bureau of Justice Statistics 1988). If we acknowledge at the outset that we are basing our estimates of juvenile violence and violence trends largely on official data sources that are inherently inaccurate for a variety of reasons, we can then assess more realistically the conclusions drawn by different investigators about such violence and violence trends among youthful offenders. Full juvenile histories are often unavailable in many jurisdictions. Sealing and expungement, two widely used methods of assuring confidentiality of records, continue to be widespread throughout the juvenile justice system (U.S. Bureau of Justice Statistics 1988). Fingerprinting of juveniles is also subject to interjurisdictional variations. Thus, accurate data gathering about the prevalence of violent crime is additionally hampered by many procedural safeguards.

Furthermore, different violence trends may be observed, reported, and interpreted, depending upon the time interval examined. For example, the percent of violent crime arrests (attributable to those under eighteen years of age) has systematically declined from 13.2 percent to 8.5 percent between 1972 and 1987 (U.S. Department of Justice 1988b). Yet, between 1978 and 1987, certain violent crimes for those under age eighteen exhibited widely divergent percentage and directional changes in arrests. Percent change *increases* were observed for forcible rape (20 percent) and aggravated assault (8.3 percent), although percent change *decreases* were observed for homicide (− 2.7 percent) and robbery (− 25.5 percent), for the years

1978–1987 (Jameison and Flanagan 1988:489). If we rely on overall arrest trends for violent crimes, focusing exclusively on those under age eighteen, then generally, arrests for violent crimes among juveniles have decreased between 1972 and 1987. However, if we select specific violent crime categories, then arrests for certain types of violent crimes among juveniles have both increased and decreased during the 1978–1987 period.

One manifestation of juvenile violence, particularly in large urban areas, is gang violence (Chicago Police Department, Gang Crimes Section 1988; Spergel 1986; Takata and Zevitz 1987). Significant media attention is directed toward juvenile gang violence, as joggers in parks and subway passengers are seemingly assaulted regularly by youth gangs. This media attention often sensationalizes juvenile violence and grossly distorts the public view of the incidence of violent crime among youths. Rogers and Mays (1987:545) acknowledge the impact of media coverage of juvenile violence on public policy. They further note that although violent crime generally includes homicide, rape, robbery, and aggravated assault, about 90 percent of all violent crimes among juveniles are robberies and aggravated assaults, committed against other juveniles; most of these crimes are also group activities.

If we use the growth and prevalence of juvenile gangs over the years as a measure of violence, then it would seem that violence, at least gang-related violence, has increased. Various surveys of public opinion in different communities confirm this. In Racine, Wisconsin, for example, 543 residents were surveyed between 1985 and 1986. About 81 percent of these respondents believed that a gang problem existed in their community, and that anywhere from three to five gangs were currently operative in the city (Takata and Zevitz 1987). However, research about delinquent gangs in other cities suggests that a substantial rise in the number of gangs is largely illusory, and that the net effect has been the application of premature and destructive strategies and ineffective public policies to combat the "gang problem" (Hagedorn 1988).

One popular view of juvenile violence is that only a small proportion of juvenile offenders actually engage in violent crimes. For instance, a study by the Youth Policy and Law Center, Inc. (1984) reported that the number of chronically violent juveniles was extremely small, accounting for only 3 percent of a sample that were arrested in three Wisconsin counties in 1980. Research reported by the National Juvenile Data Archive is generally supportive of this study (Speirs 1989). An analysis of 340,254 cases submitted to the Archive by juvenile courts in twelve states, in 1984, showed that only 6 percent of the youths referred to juvenile court were charged with one of the four violent crimes noted above (Speirs 1989:1). Furthermore, the referral rate was seven times as great for boys as it was for girls, and four times as great for nonwhites, as for whites (Speirs 1989:1).

If it is true that violent crime among juveniles is committed by a limited number of hard-core offenders, then it would seem a feasible strategy to attempt to isolate these comparatively few offenders and target them for special treatment within the juvenile justice system (Loeber and Dishion 1987). In fact, this was the primary objective of the Habitual Serious and Violent Juvenile Offender Program inaugurated by the Office of Juvenile Justice and Delinquency Prevention in 1984 (American Institutes for Research 1988). According to some experts, the most important factors that are useful for predicting violence are past violence, age, gender, race, socioeconomic status, and alcohol/drug abuse (Fisher 1984). However, there are diverse views and considerable controversy about the validity and reliability underlying clinical predictions of juvenile dangerousness and violent behavior (Fisher 1984).

It is our opinion that while the sheer volume of juvenile violence has increased throughout the United States over the years, the rate of violence among juveniles has fluctuated considerably. In fact, in recent years, the juvenile violence rate appears to have plateaued (excepting yearly fluctuations in arrest statistics for specific violent crime categories). Further, the "small core of violent offenders" argument is convincing (Mathias 1984).

From all outward appearances, it would seem that juvenile courts in the past have reflected a tendency to deal directly with chronic and violent offenders, rather than to pass them along through waivers to criminal courts. On the basis of statistics gathered by the Violent Juvenile Offender Research and Development Program during 1982–1983, for instance, a sample of 114 offenders averaged 10.5 delinquency petitions and 5.7 delinquency adjudications (Hartstone and

Hansen 1984). This suggests considerable recidivism among violent offenders in the same juvenile courts, with little, if any, effort made by judges to transfer these juveniles to criminal courts.

As already noted, there is an additional dimension that should be considered when making qualitative evaluations of delinquent behavior. While offenses may be violent and/or dangerous, they must also be evaluated according to their seriousness. While all violent crimes are serious crimes, it does not follow that all serious crimes are violent ones. Thus, offense seriousness may be measured not only by victim injuries and physical harm, but also in psychological and monetary terms. Juvenile drug dealers may not be violent offenders, yet their behavior is definitely serious. It is serious because of the potential harm it may inflict upon others, financially, physically, and psychologically. Juvenile judges and prosecutors must address each of these offense dimensions equally when making waiver decisions.

DELINQUENCY REDEFINED

Formulating a definition of delinquency acceptable to all justice professionals and criminologists is a difficult task, if not an impossible one. There are interjurisdictional variations in delinquency definitions. Furthermore, law enforcement officers may exercise discretion and warn certain juveniles informally rather than arrest them. Any delinquent conduct must be assessed in a variety of sociocultural contexts.

Social conceptions and definitions of delinquency are comparatively more subjective than legal ones. Frequently, deviant behavior or acts are regarded by many adults as indicators of delinquency, although no statute exists prohibiting these deviant behaviors or acts. A teenager might be considered "delinquent" by a neighbor if she plays loud rock music late at night and if the neighbor is trying to sleep. Wearing certain types of clothing or jewelry may "type" particular juveniles as delinquent, although no laws prohibit the offending clothing or jewelry. Guilt by association may be implied, if a juvenile "hangs out" with other juveniles who are known or believed to be delinquent.

Generally, the legal definition of delinquency encompasses conduct by those under eighteen years of age, an age standard applicable in most jurisdictions, and where such conduct would otherwise be a crime if committed by adults in those same jurisdictions. Again, law enforcement officers may decide to relabel juvenile acts according to their present inclinations. They may label "attempted breaking and entering" as "curfew violation" or "loitering," or they may label "attempted rape" simply as an argument between the youthful couple. However, as we have seen, the removal of various status offenses from juvenile court jurisdiction has deprived the courts and officers of some discretionary power. Now it is likely that previously innocent or less serious behavior such as "loitering" may be relabeled by police as "attempted breaking and entering" or "possession of burglary tools."

As will be seen in Chapter 2, several options are available to prosecutors and judges when deciding whether to charge juveniles with specific offenses. These decisions are influenced by many factors, and often, lesser-included offenses may be substituted for more serious charges or allegations. In many cases, charges against juveniles are dismissed altogether in favor of some less punitive noninstitutional option. This is usually accomplished through plea bargaining, or negotiations between a juvenile's defense attorney and the prosecution for leniency in exchange for the youth's compliance with informal probation or some other out-of-court conditional option (Rudman et al. 1986).

In many jurisdictions, status offenses may fall within the purview of juvenile judges, together with delinquent offenses. Attempts have been made to remove status offenses from the jurisdiction of juvenile courts through deinstitutionalization or divestiture. Weeding out the less serious offenders from the more serious ones is an important classificatory step toward greater equity in adjudications and the administration of punishments. Not everyone supports deinstitutionalization, however. Some believe that justice will not be served if there is no formal punishment or public accounting for wrongdoing, regardless of whether it is criminal or noncriminal conduct. Thus, unruly or incorrigible children, truants, runaways, and smoking, liquor, drug violators often share the same adjudicatory fate as those who have committed homicide, rape, robbery, burglary, and other crimes.

There is a great amount of "hidden delinquency." Many juvenile offenders are never caught and punished for their delinquent conduct. We know that for many youthful offenders, their rates of offending and reoffending decline with advancing years (Greenwood 1986). It is entirely possible for many juveniles to reach adulthood and escape punishment altogether, even though they may have been chronic, violent, habitual, and serious offenders at an earlier point in time. We do not know how much delinquency goes undetected but, on the basis of self-reports from juveniles, the amount of undetected crime seems substantial (Burchard and Burchard 1987; Menard 1987).

Jurisdictional Shifts and Trends

During the last several decades, the juvenile justice system has undergone a type of metamorphosis, as alleged juvenile offenders have acquired additional rights almost commensurate with their adult counterparts. The general nature of juvenile justice reform, particularly as it pertains to a reorganization, or restructuring of juvenile courts, is toward greater bureaucratization (Sutton 1985). However, this should not be interpreted as sweeping national reform in the treatment of juveniles (Sutton 1985).

Also, juvenile justice reform has progressed at uneven rates in every jurisdiction. Some jurisdictions have been reluctant to change their juvenile codes and legal structures. Various community agencies and interest groups have been instrumental in either fostering or preventing the rapid assimilation of juvenile justice reforms by different jurisdictions (Albanese 1985; Pindur and Wells 1985; Sutton 1985). Not all jurisdictions have alternative resolution mechanisms for resolving disputes among delinquents and their victims, for example (Fine 1984). Not all jurisdictions are agreed on the precise division of labor that should prevail between juvenile courts and community welfare agencies.

Increasingly, private interests have encroached into the juvenile justice system, particularly in the correctional area. These privatization interests have offered helpful, constructive, and economical alternatives to public detention of juveniles, but their intrusion into the public sector has further complicated an already complicated juvenile justice system. Questions arise concerning the issue of accountability. Should the state punish juvenile offenders? Will private enterprise encourage greater institutionalization of youthful offenders? How will private interests fulfill their responsibilities to detained offenders, and what mechanisms will ensure their account-ability in relation to the public sector?

Increased juvenile detention facility admissions have created chronic overcrowding in these institutions, commensurate with prison and jail overcrowding for adults (Reuterman and Hughes 1984). Some researchers cite increasing numbers of children under the age of ten coming to the attention of juvenile courts, when such courts are designed primarily to meet the needs of teenagers (Sametz 1984). Limited resources in many jurisdictions and no funding or underfunding of various community-based public and private pro-grams make it difficult for certain jurisdictions to accommodate the diverse needs of youths over such a broad range (Sametz 1984).

As drugs become more pervasive in American culture, the nature of juvenile offending is gradually changing. Increasingly associated with violent offenses among juveniles are drug and alcohol abuse (Fisher 1984; Hartstone and Hansen 1984); as evidenced by an in-creased incidence of juvenile suicides, growing numbers of clinically psychotic youths, and particularly aggressive behavior against family members (Alessi et al. 1984; Kriesman and Siden 1982; Youth Policy and Law Center 1984). These developments have exacerbated exist-ing problems associated with managing the growing population of youthful offenders and coordinating the right types of programs for them, either institutionally or noninstitutionally.

For over nine decades, the juvenile justice system has proceeded largely according to the general doctrine of *parens patriae*—which has been described by some authors as the "bedrock foundation justifying the juvenile courts' intervention in the lives of children who violate certain statutory edicts" (Watkins 1987). A persuasive argument is that the "family model" of juvenile justice (couched in the context of parens patriae) has, in effect, promised more than it can deliver. Watkins (1987) observes that the original "child savers" failed to foresee the inevitable conflict between the rehabilitative dogma of parens patriae and the social, political, and economic forces of today's culture that promote "just deserts." Thus, Watkins (1987) notes, juvenile laws and the authority of juvenile courts have not only failed, but have been, in turn, undermined by and then allied with political, social, and economic forces at war with the rehabili-tative ideal characteristic of early juvenile jurisprudence.

As juvenile courts have become more "criminalized" through the intervention of "due process," the Bill of Rights, and greater prosecutorial presence in juvenile court proceedings, the court's functions have gradually gravitated away from meeting the "real needs" of children, and toward criminal prosecutions (Feld 1987a; Laub and MacMurray 1987). (Chapter 5 explores juvenile rights in detail.) Although the juvenile court traditionally has been a civil proceeding, various types of court reforms, sentencing changes, evidentiary standards, and modifications of juvenile rights are propelling it toward a more criminal format. With some degree of regularity, proposals are advanced by different professionals to unify our court systems and combine juvenile and criminal actions into one consistent process. Opponents to court unification claim that the system of special courts for young people should be preserved, although they too, favor certain reforms (Springer 1987). Often these reforms center around greater accountability for one's actions, regardless of age. The "just deserts" philosophy is quite prominent today in many juvenile court trends.

Community Welfare Agencies and Juvenile Courts

In part because of the diverse needs of juvenile offenders and the efforts of the courts and others to separate them according to their dangerousness, seriousness, or habitual behavior—community-based agencies, both public and private, have emerged to accommodate certain of these offenders and provide necessary services for them. Diversion, probation, parole, and other strategies used to manage this growing juvenile offender population has encouraged a crude division of labor between juvenile courts and communities. Informal, unofficial probation, or participation in individualized programs (e.g., learning disabilities and handicaps) has stimulated a greater demand for services and special needs operations that can complement the actions of juvenile courts and more formalized juvenile processing (Sikorski and McGee 1986; Stewart et al. 1986).

The rehabilitation–"just deserts" philosophical tension has prompted a greater alliance between juvenile courts and community-based services. As more juvenile judges impose conditional sentences on those juveniles adjudicated as delinquent—community involvement is necessarily intensified—as more agencies assume responsibilities for monitoring and managing community service, compliance with restitution orders, and intensive supervised probation programs (Challeen 1986). Acts aimed at transforming the juvenile justice system into a more accountable system, such as the Model Delinquency Act and the Model Disobedient Children's Act, hold both youths and agencies accountable for acts and treatments administered to remedy errant behavior (Rossum et al. 1987).

Fulfilling these objectives requires greater community-court interaction. Increasingly popular are day treatment programs and nonsecure residential facilities, as less formal punishments for youthful offenders. Rubin (1988) recommends that whenever juvenile judges place youths in such programs or facilities an accompanying restitution order should be provided, and the community agencies themselves should be held to a high standard of accountability to the juvenile court in order to ensure compliance with these restitution orders.

Both legal and extralegal variables (e.g., gender, race, and social class) interact to influence adjudicatory dispositions in contemporary juvenile courts (Shelden and Horvath 1987). A major shift in the selection and administration of punishments has obligated many juvenile courts to reassess their priorities and functions. In Hawaii, for instance, current waiver practices place considerable discretion in the hands of juvenile judges, although a movement is occurring toward automatic or mandatory waiver procedures for specific serious offenses (Hawaii Criminal Justice Commission 1986).

Some professionals regard the jailing of juveniles as "cruel and unusual punishment" (Carlson 1987). Some states, such as Tennessee, Oregon, and Colorado, have set forth specific standards whereby youths may be confined in secure detention facilities. In Oregon, for example, a state-funded "broker of detention services" serves the needs of juvenile offenders in rural counties where detention facilities are either sparse or nonexistent (Carlson 1987). Hospitals and barracks are used in certain Colorado communities, where sheriff's deputies and off-duty police officers watch over juveniles for 48-hour periods (Carlson 1987).

Although pre-sentence investigation reports are still most visible and widely used as pre-sentencing information for judges dealing with convicted criminals, it is clear that juvenile judges must increasingly rely on independently prepared reports from intake officers and other juvenile court officials, in deciding a youth's ultimate disposition. Greater cooperation between the courts and community-based services is needed, especially in view of publicly expressed attitudes, in opinion polls, which favor sentencing juveniles to special treatment programs or counseling in lieu of incarceration (Steinhart 1988). Judges must be apprised of existing community services as possible sentencing alternatives, and they must be sensitive to the needs of both status offenders and more serious juvenile offenders (Tittle and Curran 1988).

Incarcerating the most serious juvenile offenders is unlike incarcerating adult offenders. Juvenile correctional facilities must give greater attention to educational and vocational programs. The average length of detention in secure juvenile facilities is considerably shorter than the length of incarceration in adult correctional facilities. Thus, intervention programs, especially educational and vocational programs, must be modified and streamlined to equip affected youths with various skills and competencies that will enable them to be more productive members of their communities, when released.

Drug treatment programs are an increasingly important element in community-based services. However, such programs require special staffing and have other unique dimensions that many jurisdictions cannot afford (Steinhart 1988). Child abuse and neglect cases often require out-of-home placement and special treatment or planning (National Council of Juvenile and Family Court Judges 1986). Despite the obvious need for community services such as those already noted, many juvenile judges will continue to exercise personalized discretion as a means of enhancing their legitimation and continuing the flow of resources to their courts (Hasenfeld and Cheung 1985). These personalized decisions often may be at odds with the best interests and needs of juveniles who appear in juvenile courts.

New Jurisdictional Boundaries and the Creation of New Law Violations

A greater range of rights is being extended to juveniles in juvenile courts (Dale 1987). At the same time, punishment and treatment of especially chronic and severe delinquents has shifted more toward adult court processing, through transfers or waivers (Miller 1986b). Status offenders have been filtered out of many juvenile justice systems toward various community social services (Miller 1986b). These shifts are consistent with the "just deserts" philosophy that currently dominates many juvenile justice proceedings (Schneider and Schram 1986; Springer 1987).

As greater numbers of youthful offenders are waived to criminal court jurisdiction, questions arise about whether transferred juveniles are fully capable of accepting the responsibilities associated with these criminal proceedings (Metchik 1987b). For instance, how likely are youths to fail to attend one or more scheduled appearances that often extend over many months, in criminal courts? Can reliable predictive criteria be established that will enable officials to distinguish those who will appear each time, from those who will not? How will such criteria differ from those typically used by pretrial service agencies in making release recommendations for adults (Metchik 1987a, 1987b; Tracy 1987)?

Within the juvenile justice system itself, "get tough" measures include greater use of detention, as well as greater use of waivers to criminal courts. Overcrowding of juvenile correctional facilities is a "given," but it is a problem that must be reckoned with and resolved. Front-end and back-end solutions include greater use of probation and parole. Placing population "caps", or limits on detention facilities in various states sets into motion several system adjustments and responses that impact in various ways upon the entire juvenile justice system (Fox and Viegas 1987).

Diverting less serious youths from the juvenile justice system to community-based services, including nonsecure residential programs with electronic monitoring, places a new set of constraints upon affected juveniles. Many community-based programs are unsure of the degree of sanctioning power they possess when youths fail to comply with program requirements or rules. Also, these agencies, facilities, and personnel are unfamiliar with changing laws pertaining to juveniles and the different kinds of liabilities they incur as community interventions.

Preadjudication detention of juveniles is lawful in all jurisdictions. However, these juveniles transferred to criminal courts are now in the unenviable position of being placed in jails and other detention facilities with adults—where the risk of sexual assault is great and the criminogenic atmosphere is intense. Changing laws in many jurisdictions mandate automatic transfers of juveniles to criminal courts. In New York, for instance, the Juvenile Offender Law passed in 1978 provides for automatic transfers of juveniles to criminal court, where specific serious offenses are alleged (Singer 1985). A similar automatic transfer provision has been enacted in Illinois (Reed 1983). Economic and logistical assessments of these automatic transfer laws suggest that youths are retained for longer periods, awaiting trial, and that the services ordinarily available to them in juvenile courts are simply nonexistent in adult proceedings. This loss of valuable services and the greater detention time indicate that the cost of mandatory transfer far outstrips its potential financial and social benefits (Reed 1983).

A strong critic of the criminalization of juvenile courts contends that many current administrative assumptions and operations are virtually indistinguishable from those of adult criminal courts (Feld 1984a). At the same time, procedural safeguards available in juvenile courts are less adequate than those extended alleged adult offenders in criminal courts. Feld (1984a) says that juveniles literally have the "worst of both worlds."

PUBLIC POLICY AND JUVENILES

The juvenile justice system has been criticized as consisting, in many instances, of a patchwork of procedures, institutions, and agencies that are only loosely coordinated to deal ineffectively with youthful offenders (Georgia Commission on Juvenile Justice 1985). The fact that community-based services exist in some jurisdictions to meet the special needs of youthful offenders does not automatically mean that these services will be utilized effectively by judges and others, when adjudicating juveniles (Conti et al. 1984). The lack of coordination and planning that typifies juvenile courts in more than a few jurisdictions, also typifies community-based agencies and services.

Juvenile justice and court reforms have been stimulated by diverse interests (Fine 1984; Sutton 1985). A strong rehabilitation contingent continues to see the juvenile court as mainly serving a treatment function, although increasing bureaucratization of juvenile courts has intensified the demand for greater juvenile accountability and severity in punishment (Ito 1984; Sametz 1984).

In most jurisdictions, juveniles are not entitled to a jury trial as a matter of right, although the "beyond a reasonable doubt" criminal standard is now used in most adjudication proceedings. There is abundant evidence of discrimination in juvenile court proceedings—especially based on race, gender, and socioeconomic status (Tittle and Curran 1988). The perennial conflict between due process and parens patriae has not abated, and it continues to adversely affect the treatment of juveniles among jurisdictions (Dale 1987).

Public opinion polls continue to reflect the idea that most citizens regard the juvenile court as essential, and many of these respondents believe that rehabilitation should be the court's primary goal (Steinhart 1988). Interestingly, many citizens also believe that current measures of offense seriousness are inadequate, and that many juveniles who are sentenced receive punishments that are too lenient (Harris 1988).

An analysis of the literature pertaining to juvenile justice reforms suggests strongly that juvenile courts should rely increasingly on punishments and sanctions that meet juveniles' abilities and needs. Some investigators emphasize greater use of community-based treatment, restitution, diversion, and intensive supervised probation (Sametz 1984; Seljan 1983). An effective partnership needs to be established between juvenile courts, community agencies, and business interests (National Council of Juvenile and Family Court Judges 1986). Some views combine punishment with pragmatism: where punishments may be imposed together with treatment, education, and rehabilitation, after justice has been served (Springer 1987).

The National Council of Juvenile and Family Court Judges (1985) has indicated that the key to solving the problems of juvenile justice is in establishing an effective partnership of courts and public agencies, with the full involvement of business, labor, private agencies, and citizen volunteers. Also essential is an emphasis on delinquency prevention and a sensitivity to the rights of children and their families. The Council outlines specific policy recommendations that include judges' roles, court procedures, detecting, reporting and evaluating child abuse, out-of-home placement, treatment and planning, and prevention.

Currently, there are variable dispositional options available to juvenile judges in most jurisdictions. These options include unofficial probation, referral to specific community agencies, warnings and case dismissals, waivers, detention hearings, and conditional punishments, such as community service and restitution (Stewart et al.

1986). In some jurisdictions, such as Columbia County, Georgia, peer juries exist as essential parts of diversion programs, to hear charges against youths and adjudicate them according to the evidence presented (Reichel and Seyfrit 1984; Seyfrit et al. 1987). These juries consist of five jurors under age seventeen who are trained by the juvenile court staff. A list of eligible youths is used for making these juror selections. Available evidence suggests that these peer juries are quite capable of dispensing appropriate punishments in nonserious as well as serious cases (Seyfrit et al. 1987).

Currently, the juvenile justice system is in a state of flux, with little consistency among jurisdictions. The strong message emanating from experts is that juvenile justice must be predictable, but not necessarily harsh (Conrad 1983). A continuing concern is reducing recidivism among juvenile offenders, and determining the right types of interventions that work most effectively to reduce a juvenile's propensity to reoffend (Nagoshi 1986; Rydell 1986). Many researchers believe that early intervention in school settings may be beneficial in deterring youths from committing status offenses or engaging in criminal activity (Hawkins and Lamb 1987; Kimbrough 1986).

Better classification systems must be devised to segregate juvenile offenders more effectively, and to selectively channel only the most serious youths into the juvenile justice mainstream (Karraker 1988). Some researchers believe that decisions to transfer youths to criminal court are often reflections of the juvenile court's unwillingness to accept alternative interventions available in communities, or to consider less formal adjudicatory strategies (Grisso et al. 1988). However, a significant segment of a concerned public endorses greater use of transfers, especially for the most serious, chronic, and dangerous youthful offenders (Metchik 1987a). In Chapter 2, the juvenile justice system is outlined in terms of form and function. Several dispositional options are presented that guide juvenile judges in their adjudications of youths.

SUMMARY

The rehabilitative, treatment-centered philosophy that has dominated the criminal justice system for the first half of the twentieth century has gradually given way to the "just deserts," or justice philosophy. The justice philosophy is associated with harsher punishments, and administering penalties for offenders according to the seriousness of their crimes. The "get tough" movement has prompted the trend toward "just deserts." The "get tough" movement has also pervaded the juvenile justice system.

In the last few decades, a massive transformation of the juvenile justice system has occurred. Numerous reforms have been observed in juvenile rights, juvenile court organization and operations, adjudication and sentencing, and modifications of the penalties available to judges as sentencing options. One increasingly important option available to judges is the transfer of more serious, or chronic juveniles to adult criminal courts.

Juveniles most likely to be transferred to criminal court are those persistent offenders who have committed offenses that would be crimes, if committed by adults. A distinction is made between status offenses and delinquency: status offenses are not criminal acts, they include runaway behavior, curfew violation, and truancy. Delinquency is any act committed by a person under a certain age (usually eighteen) that would be a crime if committed by an adult. There are differences among jurisdictions about how delinquency is defined. Social and legal definitions of delinquency differ, and sometimes classification problems occur, as officials attempt to segregate youthful offenders according to offense seriousness. A movement has begun to remove status offenses from juvenile court jurisdiction, largely because of their nonseriousness. Not everyone agrees that deinstitutionalization of status offenses is a worthwhile strategy for dealing with youthful offenders, although there are merits to deinstitutionalization.

The amount of delinquency in the United States is unknown. Almost every official statistical compilation is flawed, and it is likely that most estimates of delinquency are underestimates. Violent crime among juveniles rose during the 1970s, but during the 1980s it appeared to level off. One reaction to the public to violent juvenile offense behavior is to transfer these juveniles to adult criminal courts where a broader range of more stringent punishments, including the death penalty, may be administered.

The juvenile justice system suffers from many of the problems of its adult counterpart, the criminal justice system. Juvenile detention facilities are typically overcrowded, and no particular intervention strategy seems acceptable to all juvenile justice professionals. Because the juvenile justice system is fragmented and diverse among jurisdictions, various professionals have advocated greater harmony and cooperative effort between juvenile courts and community-based agencies, to better serve the needs of youthful offenders. Consistent policy decisions are needed; and better definitions of offense seriousness must be devised.

NOTES

1. It is significant to note that many U.S. jurisdictions continue to handle juvenile matters through family courts, courts of common pleas, chancery courts, magistrate's courts, and assorted trial courts.

2. Prosecutors for the U.S. government have broad discretionary powers about when certain youthful offenders are prosecuted for their offenses. For instance, one defendant was charged with crimes two weeks after his twenty-first birthday, although the crimes alleged occurred before his eighteenth birthday. A federal appellate court concluded, "the (defendant), who was not charged until two weeks after his twenty-first birthday, was not entitled to protection of Juvenile Delinquency Act, although defendant allegedly committed crimes before his eighteenth birthday and could have been prosecuted earlier but, through no fault of his own, was indicted after his twenty-first birthday." *United States v. Hoo*, 825 F. 2d 667 (1987).

3. One example is Ohio, where a delinquent child is, among other things, a child who violates a lawful court order (Ohio Revised Code 1987; Whitehead and Lab 1990:3).

CHAPTER 2

An Overview of the Juvenile Justice System

In some ways it is awkward to talk about a juvenile justice system—and there are at least two reasons for this. First, there is some debate over whether a criminal justice system exists (see, e.g., Moore 1976; Neubauer 1988). If there is not an adult criminal justice *system*, then in all likelihood, there is not a juvenile justice *system* either. Second, if there is a criminal justice system, it is possible that juvenile justice agencies are simply a part of that system, not apart from the system. The following section will discuss those agencies that distinctly process juvenile offenders, and those that process juveniles and adults.

THE JUVENILE JUSTICE SYSTEM

One criticism regarding the use of the term "system" is that it implies a coordinated effort, with agreement on purposes. While there is a conspicuous lack of coordination in the juvenile justice system, for explanatory purposes juvenile justice will be considered a system, albeit one where the individual components sometimes work at cross purposes, or at counter purposes. These components include law enforcement agencies (the police), courts, and correctional agencies and organizations. Figure 2.1 illustrates the classic flow diagram of justice system processes, including, in the lower portion, the specialized juvenile justice operations.

The Police

In the area of law enforcement, there is little differentiation between juvenile and adult offenders. Police officers are responsible for arresting law violators, whether they are juveniles or adults. For the most part, the procedures employed by the police vary little as the result of a suspect's age. There are some differences, however, and these variations will be explained.

When making arrests, most police methods are identical for juveniles and adults. After an arrest occurs, police procedures begin to diverge based on the age of the offender. These distinctions include fingerprinting and photographing of suspects and interrogation techniques (Davis 1980: 344–363; Hahn, 1978:254–57).

Based on the National Advisory Committee's (1976:221–23) Standard 5.12 "Guidelines for Fingerprinting, Photographing and Other Identification," most states prohibit routine fingerprinting and photographing of juvenile suspects. For example, while not a blanket prohibition on fingerprinting and photographing of juvenile suspects, New Mexico Statutes Annotated, Section 32–1–27, I. provides that "A child alleged to be or adjudicated as a child in need of supervision [status offender] or a child under the age of thirteen alleged or adjudicated to be a delinquent child shall not be fingerprinted or photographed for identification purposes without obtaining a court order." This is one area where the procedures for juveniles and adults depart substantially. In most instances, with adult arrestees, fingerprinting and photographing are done as routine booking procedures. When adult suspects are brought to jail, they are fingerprinted and photographed as a part of the identification and documentation process, and little thought is given to this procedure. However, the standards recommend, and most state juvenile codes provide, that these identification techniques be employed only (1) for investigative purposes (i.e., to establish a suspect's presence at the scene of a crime), and (2) to determine the individual's true identity and age. Such processes, however, are to be done only under court order and for temporary use, not for purposes of developing a permanent criminal record.

The fear, in handling juvenile suspects, is that such routine "criminal" processing would emphasize or increase the stigma associated with formal justice system processing. Therefore, police operations reflect the original conception of the juvenile justice system: procedures should be confidential, nonadversarial, and, to the extent possible, nonstigmatizing.

The Juvenile Court

It is fairly accurate to characterize the juvenile court as the centerpiece of the juvenile justice system—since in some ways, once the court was created, the "system" developed around it. The juvenile court did not spring suddenly full-blown onto the American justice scene. In fact, it is possible to view the juvenile court as the culmination of several centuries of jurisprudential evolution; (Rubin 1985, 1989; U.S. Department of Justice 1988b).

In the United States two particular events substantially contributed to the creation of a separate juvenile court. First, the Industrial Revolution of the mid-to-late 1800s transformed America from a rural, agrarian economy to one increasingly based on manufacturing and heavy industry. Along with the Industrial Revolution, the United States experienced much immigration from Europe (both eastern and western European countries) and from Asia. These immigrants provided labor, often at the lowest possible prices, to fuel the movement toward an industrial economy. These immigrants also brought with them children who often roamed the streets of the industrial cities. Concern over immigrant children committing crime and living dissolute lives led many progressive reformers to seek ways to aid these children (see Davis 1980:3–15).

The second major event, therefore, was the Progressive movement (Bartollas 1990). These individuals and groups were much concerned about the quality of life in America's cities, and from these efforts evolved what has come to be known as the "child saving movement" (see, Cullen et al. 1983). While there are various interpretations of the "child savers'" motives (see, e.g., Platt 1977; Schlossman 1977), clearly there were philanthropic societies and associations in many cities given over to improving the lives of lower-class immigrant

Figure 2.1
A general view of the criminal justice system

This chart seeks to present a simple yet comprehensive view of the movement of cases through the criminal justice system. Procedures in individual jusisdictions may vary from the pattern shown here. The differing weights of line indicate the relative volumes of cases disposed of at various points in the system, but this is only suggestive since no nationwide data of this sort exists.

Courts

Information 5

Police   **Prosecution**

Undetected Crimes

Unsolved or Not Arrested

Released Without Prosecution

Charges Dropped or Dismissed

Crimes Observed by the Police

Investigation 1

Arrest

Book- 2 ing

Initial 3 Appear- ance

Prelimin- 4 ary Hearing

Felonies

Grand

Refusal to Indict

Crime

Crimes Reported to the Police

Misdemeanors

Information 5

Petty Offenses

Unreported Crimes

Release or Station Adjustment

Released

Police 10 Juvenile Unit

Intake Hearing 11

Non-Police Referrals

Juvenile Offenses

1 May continue until trial.
2 Administrative record of arrest. First step at which temporary release on bail may be available.
3 Before magistrate, commissioner, or justice of peace. Formal notice of charge, advice of rights. Bail set. Summary trials for petty offenses usually conducted here without further processing

4 Preliminary testing of evidence against defendant. Charge may be reduced. No separate preliminary hearing for misdemeanors in some systems.
5 Charge filed by prosecutor on basis of information submitted by police or citizens. Alternative to grand jury indictment often used in felonies, almost always in misdemeanors.
6 Reviews whether Government evidence sufficient to justify trial. Some States have no grand jury system, others seldom use it.

Figure 2.1(continued)

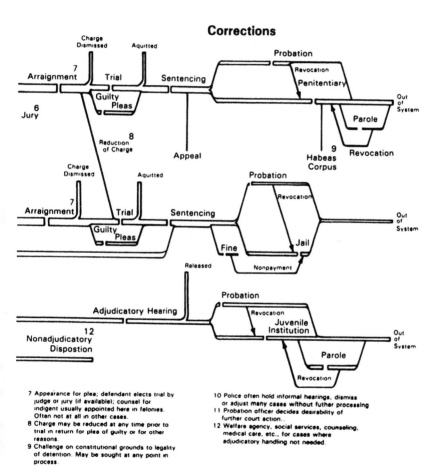

Corrections

7 Appearance for plea; defendant elects trial by judge or jury (if available); counsel for indigent usually appointed here in felonies. Often not at all in other cases.
8 Charge may be reduced at any time prior to trial in return for plea of guilty or for other reasons.
9 Challenge on constitutional grounds to legality of detention. May be sought at any point in process.

10 Police often hold informal hearings, dismiss or adjust many cases without futher processing
11 Probation officer decides desirability of further court action.
12 Welfare agency, social services, counseling, medical care, etc., for cases where adjudicatory handling not needed.

children—especially those coming into contact with the law (Vito and Wilson 1985).

Apparently there were two explicit motivating factors in the child saving movement: (1) a desire to instill "proper" civic and moral values in youngsters, and (2) a concomitant desire to mitigate the law's often harsh treatment of children. It was a common practice, in fact, for courts not to distinguish between children and adults in determining their degree of culpability, as well as the severity and place of their punishment (Rubin 1985b:52). This meant, of course, that children were punished commensurate with adults and, at times in the same prisons and jails.

As a result of the courts' harsh treatment of children, "child savers" such as Jane Addams and Julia Lathrop felt strongly that age should be a mitigating circumstance before the law. Thus, a unique blending of jurisprudence and the social welfare philosophy resulted in the founding of the juvenile court in Cook County, Illinois in 1899 (Binder 1979).

The juvenile court, as it was originally conceived, was to have a number of distinctive features. First, juvenile court proceedings were to be marked by different terminology than adult proceedings. Absent were warrants, trials, and sentences, and in their place were petitions, hearings, and dispositions (Binder and Binder 1982; Bortner 1988). Children would not be found guilty. Instead, they would be adjudicated delinquent and viewed as in need of the court's help.

Second, adjudication hearings were to be *private*. Unlike adult criminal trials, delinquency hearings were not open to the public, a feature emphasizing their rehabilitative, nonstigmatizing nature (Cox and Conrad 1987:114–15). This often meant that both the public and representatives of the news media were excluded. No publicity surrounded these hearings and no publication was made of the names of accused delinquents.

Third, hearings were to be *informal*. This informality was characterized by the lack of judges' robes and a trial bench. Hearings in many courts were conducted around conference tables where the prevailing question was: "How can we help this child?" The assumption was that *all* parties present were acting on behalf of the child. Also, many of the formal rules of procedure and evidence were conspicuously absent. This particular manifestation of informality caused problems for the juvenile courts, which resulted in appellate court reviews of juvenile procedures, beginning in the late-1960s.

Finally, delinquency proceedings were to be *nonadversarial*. One of the guiding theoretical principles of Anglo-American law is that there are two adversaries in any case, their interests are in opposition, and one wins and the other loses. Juvenile cases, however, were envisioned as nonadversarial in that the child was not supposed to be in jeopardy, and all parties were present and acting "in the best interests of the child." Although the reality was that children were very much in jeopardy, and many were deprived of their liberty without due process of law (see, Binder 1979; *In re Gault* 1967; *In re Winship* 1970; and *Kent v. United States* 1966).

Between 1966 and 1975 many substantial changes occurred in the legal environment of the juvenile court. The Supreme Court's "due process revolution" spilled over into the juvenile courts, and delinquents were extended most (but not all) of the due process rights provided adult criminal defendants (Rubin 1985b:273–75). Expanding due process protections changed the fundamentally informal and nonadversarial nature of the juvenile court. Attorneys were used with increasing frequency, and the distinction between adult courts and juvenile courts became less clear. As a result of such diminished distinctiveness, some critics have called for an end to separate adult and juvenile courts (see Mays 1980).

Juvenile court procedures have contributed to change from the mid-1970s through the 1980s, and there have been two lines of criticism. One group of people, properly characterized as modern "child savers," believe that juvenile courts have been and continue to be entirely too punitive. These people want to reaffirm the rehabilitative philosophy (Cullen and Gilbert 1982; Weisheit and Alexander 1988). The second group, while not necessarily larger, has been vocal in its criticisms of juvenile court leniency. These "crime control" critics have been heard, and the result has been that the general nature of juvenile court changes has been in the direction of more punitive or "just deserts" oriented dispositions. One indicator of punitiveness—transfers of juveniles to adult courts—is the focus of this book.

Juvenile Corrections

Juvenile corrections can be thought of as comprised of three segments: probation, incarceration, and parole (or aftercare). The unique feature of juvenile probation, however, is that unlike adult

Table 2.1
Number of state and local agencies performing probation or parole functions, by level of government, September 1, 1976

Level of government	Agency function[1]				Parole authorities	
	Probation		Parole			
	Adult probation	Juvenile probation	Adult parole	Juvenile parole		
	number	per-cent	number	per-cent	number	per-cent	number	per-cent	number	per-cent

Level of government	number	per-cent	number	per-cent	number	per-cent	number	per-cent	number	per-cent
State -local total..	1,929	100	2,126	100	1,154	100	1,221	100	65	100
State..........................	1,087	56	916	43	984	85	992	81	64	98
county......................	788	41	1,167	55	165	15	227	19	-	-
municipal.................	54	3	43	2	5	(Z)	2	(Z)	1	2

Source: Law Enforcement Assistance Administration, State and Local Probation and Parole Systems. Washington, DC: U.S. Department of Justice, 1978, p. 2.

[1] Agencies having multiple functions are counted in more than one column.

- Represents zero.

(Z) Percent rounds to zero.

probation it is often a judicial function. Adult probation and parole offices, typically, are part of the state corrections apparatus. In other words—they are executive functions. By contrast, in many states juvenile probation offices are attached to the juvenile courts and the juvenile court judges are responsible for selecting juvenile probation officers (JPOs), especially the chief JPO. Table 2.1 illustrates the organizational differences between juvenile and adult probation offices.

In some ways, juvenile correctional facilities are relatively recent innovations in criminal justice, most have existed for about 100 years. However, some of the precursors of correctional institutions existed even before there were juvenile courts. For example, in 1825 the first house of refuge was opened in New York City by the Society for the Prevention of Pauperism (Finckenauer 1984; Roberts 1989). This facility and others like it first appeared in the 1820s to the 1850s, and were designed to house children who were orphaned, abandoned, or destitute. Also included in the populations of houses of refuge were children who were law violators.

These houses of refuge and similar facilities often were operated by private philanthropies and religious groups. They sought to instill in their residents "appropriate" (middle-class) values relating to discipline, hard work, and education (Simonsen and Gordon 1982). Early private involvement in juvenile corrections set the tone for programs to follow (Lerman 1984). The guiding philosophy behind these early institutions (one which has carried over to modern juvenile corrections) was regeneration, restoration, or more commonly *rehabilitation*.

Modern correctional programs fall broadly into two categories: *noninstitutional* and *institutional* (Roberts 1989). Noninstitutional, or community-based, programs include arrangements such as traditional probation and parole and a variety of other diversion and nonincarcerative alternatives. Institutional corrections, while employing facilities with a range of security levels, is frequently thought of in terms of state training schools for both male and female adjudicated delinquents. In most instances, these institutions are simply juvenile prisons. They detain youngsters in secure settings for some predetermined amount of time or until they are "cured."

Currently, the trend in juvenile corrections is toward fewer and smaller correctional facilities. The movement toward deinstitutionalization, especially of status offenders, has had a significant impact on secure juvenile placements (Bureau of Justice Statistics 1989; Schneider 1984a; U.S. Department of Justice 1988b). However, the decrease in secure placements has, for the most part, been offset by increases in nonsecure, community-based programs (Bureau of Justice Statistics 1986; Office of Juvenile Justice and Delinquency Prevention 1980a, 1980b; U.S. Department of Justice 1988b).

After they have been confined in a correctional facility, most youths spend some time under community supervision. It is not unusual for this process to be called parole, as in the adult system, but some states prefer to distinguish juvenile supervision by characterizing it as "aftercare."

Whatever the label, the process of community-based supervision and surveillance is essential in aiding juveniles' reintegration. Juvenile parole officers assist the youth and the family in reestablishing ties in the home, school, and neighborhood. Some effort may be made as well to help older youths find employment, job training, or to begin the process of establishing independent living arrangements (Finckenauer 1984; Trester 1981).

Juvenile parole, unlike juvenile probation, tends to be a state government function, at times operating in conjunction with adult probation and parole. Table 2.1 illustrates the differences in organizational levels of juvenile probation and parole.

INTAKE AND INTAKE DISPOSITIONS

We have now taken a brief look at the juvenile justice system. From this overview it is important to focus on three particular aspects of system processing or court procedures: the *intake process, adjudicatory hearings*, and *dispositions*. These three decision points will be explored here and in the following two sections.

Intake decisions are influenced by several distinct, but interrelated, sets of actors: police officers, juvenile probation officers or other court intake workers, and juvenile court judges. First, the police play a major role at the point of intake, by referring as many as half of the cases they encounter to the court (Rubin 1985b:93–95). In fact, the police provide the vast majority of referrals to the juvenile courts—about 75 percent in most courts (U.S. Department of Justice 1988b:78).

The initial decision made by the police and intake workers concerns whether to detain the juvenile temporarily. In most instances, suspected offenders are held only long enough to process paperwork and to contact their parents. Detention for longer periods of time is justified only when the juvenile has committed a very serious personal crime (such as homicide, rape, or armed robbery) and there is an immediate danger to the public, when the risk of flight prior to scheduled court hearings is high, or when the accused juvenile might be in danger from the public (Frazier 1989).

Just prior to, or at the same time intake workers are deciding whether to detain the juvenile, they consider what charges, if any, seem justified. In some cases the police will have a major impact on this decision. At other times, especially because of court policies or staff exigencies, intake workers or prosecutors will control the charging decision (see, Rubin 1980). In order to understand intake decision making it is necessary to examine the actors and influences that impact on the intake process.

Intake Decision Makers

Most juvenile courts have an intake staff. Depending on the size of the court, this staff can be one or more persons who decide whether a given case warrants the issuance of a petition on behalf of the child. For most of the juvenile court's history, intake decisions have been made by court workers such as juvenile probation officers. These individuals are appointed (and can be removed) at the pleasure of the judge in many jurisdictions. They are the extra eyes and ears for juvenile court judges. In some instances, the courts (i.e., the judges) have developed a specialized intake staff that is separate from the juvenile probation office.

As a result of the increasingly adversarial nature of the juvenile court, prosecuting attorneys have supplanted or supplemented the probation officers and are playing a larger role earlier in the intake process. Rubin (1980) maintains that most intake workers are inadequately prepared to make decisions concerning legal sufficiency, and that this is an evaluation that should be reserved for the prosecuting attorney. His concern, however, is that the prosecutor will eventually dominate juvenile court processes.

Intake Decision Criteria

Historically, juvenile court intake workers utilized two different sets of *factors*—social and legal—in determining the desirability of filing a delinquency petition (Rubin 1984:105, 108–9). Social factors relate to the background characteristics of the juveniles: who these youngsters are. These factors have included such things as family stability, the number of parents or guardians, the number of siblings in the family, the birth order of siblings, and the child's academic record. Legal factors relate to what the child has done. These factors include the nature of the present offense and the child's previous offense history. Of the two, social factors traditionally have played the prominent role. Recently, however, legal factors have increasingly controlled the intake process.

The importance of the intake process becomes apparent when one statistic is cited: only about 50 percent of the juveniles referred to the court by the police make it beyond the intake process (i.e., actually have a petition filed on their behalf) (Rubin 1989). This means that at intake, careful consideration must be given to both the social factors and the legal sufficiency of each case.

Intake Dispositions

Since many cases do not proceed beyond intake, it is important to consider the dispositional alternatives available to intake decision makers. As previously mentioned, one alternative is to file a petition on behalf of the child. This is normally done in three types of cases: those involving persistent offenders, those involving juveniles who have committed very serious offenses, and those where the parents are unable or unwilling to exercise appropriate control over the child (i.e., dependent or neglected children). Aside from filing a petition, however, the court has a number of other dispositional alternatives.

Unlike adult courts, juvenile courts often utilize a mechanism known as informal probation (Coffey 1975). With adults, probation is a judicial disposition imposed following adjudication, and this is true for formal behavior with juveniles as well. However, some juvenile probation offices, with the blessing of the juvenile judge, have employed informal probation in cases of very minor offenses (some types of vandalism, for example), first offenses (if they are not crimes against persons), and where it is apparent that the child has done something, but legal sufficiency has not been clearly established (Bortner 1988:107–9).

Informal probation allows the probation staff to place youngsters under some form of community supervision (typically not very intense at this stage of the process) and to serve notice on them that future law violations will result in more severe sanctions. In taking this approach, the juvenile probation staff normally holds the request for a petition (or the actual petition) in abeyance for some specified period of time (generally three to six months) to see whether there will be additional facts discovered or additional charges filed. If not, the charges will normally be dismissed, but court records concerning the nature of the child's court contact and involvement in the offense remain. One of the criticisms of informal probation is the expressed or implied coercion present during the process. In some jurisdictions informal probation and other alternatives to adjudication are handled through consent decrees. These decrees require that the child stipulate to (admit) the charges alleged, in exchange for more lenient, less formal processing. Under such circumstances due process considerations are generally suppressed or at least minimized in order to promote a rapid, informal disposition. Such offers are difficult to refuse for many children and their parents.

A variation on the theme of informal probation is the use of *diversion* programs. The principal impetus of diversion programs, as currently constituted, has been the Juvenile Justice and Delinquency Prevention Act of 1974 (Schneider 1984a, 1985; Schwartz 1989). These programs, in some ways, were resurrections of one of the juvenile court's original ideals: nonstigmatizing procedures. Diversion programs were designed to remove first offenders and relatively minor offenders from the formal adjudication process as quickly as possible to avoid the stigmatizing effects of delinquency proceedings. The results have been both gratifying and disconcerting for those reformers who so strongly advocated alternatives to the formal adjudication process (Austin and Krisberg 1982; Decker 1985; Schwartz 1989).

One intended consequence of diversion programs was the removal of large numbers of relatively minor offenders from juvenile court processing. In order to meet the treatment needs of these youths, most of whom have not faced juvenile court adjudication at this point, a variety of community-based programs and agencies have been created. Broad scale application of the diversionary philosophy has left the juvenile court dealing with the most serious cases of delinquency. In many instances, these are youngsters who do not differ substantially, in offense patterns and seriousness, from their adult counterparts.

The unintended consequence of diversion is the development of "wider, stronger, and different nets" (Austin and Krisberg 1981). In simplest terms, this means that those youngsters diverted from the formal juvenile justice system have been captured in "nets" formed by the community-based agencies (Binder 1989). If social control is viewed in its broadest terms, this means that more, not fewer, children are under some form of social control, as a result of diversionary programs. Some fear that children delabeled, through diversion, will now be relabeled through placement in community mental health and private psychiatric care facilities or treatment programs (Schneider 1984a; see also Office of Juvenile Justice and Delinquency Prevention 1980a, 1980b).

In summarizing intake decision making and dispositional options, it is important to remember that intake is not simply a "yes-no" determination. Decisions should be looked upon as occupying varying places along a continuum. The *least* severe outcome requires some action short of filing a petition—with no further action being taken on the case. The *most* severe outcome is filing a petition with the juvenile court and setting the youngster's case for an adjudicatory hearing. It should be remembered that for each option and each alternative there are consequences for the juveniles involved, especially regarding possible penalties and sanctions facing them.

ADJUDICATORY HEARINGS

Juvenile court proceedings are *bifurcated* in nature: an initial hearing is held to determine the juvenile's status (i.e., whether the accused offender is delinquent) and a second hearing (at times separated by days or weeks), to determine what should be done with the child found to be delinquent (Davis 1980:1–3). The first hearing is termed an *adjudicatory hearing*, and the second, *disposition*. This section will explore the nature of dispositional hearings, and the following section will examine dispositions and dispositional hearings.

THE NATURE OF JUVENILE COURT HEARINGS

In some ways, juvenile court hearings today very much resemble those of the juvenile court as it was originally conceived; however, there are fundamental differences. Rubin (1989:111) notes that "The juvenile court of today is a markedly different instrument than the juvenile court of two decades ago." Nowhere are the differences more apparent than in the adjudicatory process.

As previously mentioned, several appellate court decisions from the late 1960s and early 1970s had a profound impact on the ways juvenile courts operated. A few of these cases, decided by the United States Supreme Court, will illustrate the changing legal philosophy confronting the juvenile courts.

The first of the major cases decided by the Supreme Court dealing with juvenile court procedures was *Kent v. United States*, 383 U.S. 541 (1966). (Since this case deals explicitly with the issue of transfers to adult court it will be dealt with at much greater length in Chapter 3. For the time being, it is sufficient to note that *Kent* opened the door to appellate review of juvenile court procedures, even if ever so slightly.) One issue addressed by *Kent*, and one of enduring importance, was the right to representation by an attorney. Only three years before *Kent* the Supreme Court had expanded the right to counsel for adults in state felony prosecutions in the case of *Gideon v. Wainwright* (1963). Kent applied the principle to delinquency adjudications and established the right to counsel, as specified by the Sixth Amendment to the Constitution, as a requirement of fundamental due process for juvenile offenders. Some states have now added a provision for the nonwaivability of the right to counsel for juvenile suspects (see, e.g., New Mexico Statutes Annotated, Section 32–1–27 H).

The requirement of the right to counsel was to be further amplified one year after *Kent* when the Supreme Court issued an opinion in its most expansive juvenile justice case: *In re Gault*, (1967). *Gault* provided the Supreme Court with the broadest ranging and most frontal assault on juvenile procedures since the juvenile court's founding in 1899. In fact, it is fair to say that the *Gault* case challenged a number of the fundamental principles and most aspects of the way a large number of juvenile courts handled their delinquency adjudication procedures. The Court's decision left in question the nature of delinquency hearings as confidential, informal, and nonadversarial operations. Specifically, *Gault* raised constitutional questions about each of the following issues:

1. the right to notice of charges by the child and the child's parents;

2. the right to counsel as articulated in cases like *Gideon* and *Kent*;

3. the right to confront and cross-examine one's accusers;

4. protection against self-incrimination;

5. the right to a transcript of the proceedings in order to facilitate appeals if necessary;

6. the right to appeal based on errors in law.

Issues five and six were not granted by *Gault*.

While these rights are basic in any criminal prosecution, it is important to remember that historically juvenile court delinquency proceedings had not been viewed as criminal in nature. In fact, in some states, civil rules of procedure were explicitly delineated as mandatory for governing the juvenile courts.

The essential issue in *Gault* was whether constitutional due process extended to accused juvenile offenders (see Binder 1979; Binder and Binder 1982). Associate Justice Abe Fortas, writing the opinion for the Court, viewed as somewhat incredible a situation where adult criminal offenders would have constitutional rights not available to a child accused of delinquency. In one of the most famous quotes from the *Gault* decision, Fortas said, "Under our Constitution, the condition of being a boy does not justify a kangaroo court."

The lack of specificity regarding the application of criminal or civil rules of procedure was raised as a constitutional issue again in the case of *In re Winship* (1970). Prior to *Winship*, it was not uncommon for juvenile courts to employ the civil standard of proof based on the preponderance of the evidence. This meant that there was a less stringent standard of proof for establishing delinquency than would be required for proving guilt in adult courts. In *Winship* the Supreme Court held that delinquency (i.e., guilt, for adults) must be established *beyond a reasonable doubt.*

One of the major issues remaining unresolved in the wake of *Kent*, *Gault*, and *Winship* was the right to a trial by jury for juveniles. For most of the history of the juvenile court, hearings were held before a judge, and jury trials were not available. The case of *McKeiver v. Pennsylvania*, (1971) asked the Supreme Court to resolve the question of whether the right to trial by jury was constitutionally mandated in delinquency hearings. The answer, in contrast with what earlier cases might have suggested, was that jury trials are not considered an essential element of due process for juveniles. States could, if they wanted, provide jury trials, and some states do provide the option for jury trials in delinquency adjudications.[1]

Modern adjudicatory hearings for accused delinquents can be characterized in two ways. First, they still are less formal than most adult trials, and concern for the child typically dominates all aspects of the decision-making process. Second, delinquency hearings are much more formal than they traditionally were. This means that with the presence of attorneys for both sides, careful application of the rules of evidence, and a stricter weight of proof, juvenile courts are much more tightly constrained by procedural due process than they previously were. In some ways, then, this has made juvenile courts more criminal in nature.

Subsequent cases like *Davis v. Alaska* (1974) and *Breed v. Jones* (1975) have affirmed the Supreme Court's stance on the applicability of due process protections to delinquency adjudications. However, the 1980s saw very little expansion of the constitutional rights of accused juvenile offenders (of course, the same argument might be made for the rights of adult defendants).

The dilemma for some juvenile court observers is the issue of whether due process or rehabilitation will be the court's guiding philosophy. Some (e.g., Weisheit and Alexander 1988) do not believe that this has to be an either-or choice. In fact, given the bifurcated nature of juvenile court processes, it is possible to have an adjudicatory hearing governed by due process principles and dispositional hearings influenced by rehabilitative principles.

To summarize the adjudicatory processes for delinquents, two important trends have been developing simultaneously. The first that should be highlighted is the diversion of less serious offenders from the formal adjudicatory process (Schneider 1984a, 1985). This has depleted juvenile court processing of minor offenders, although it has burgeoned the numbers of more serious offenders. The second trend is the increasing formality and criminalization of delinquency hearings. When these two trends are considered simultaneously, one conclusion is that the distinction between juvenile court processes and adult criminal trials is increasingly obscured. This decreasing distinctiveness is reinforced somewhat by the dispositional outcomes imposed by the juvenile courts as well.

DISPOSITIONAL OPTIONS

Juvenile court judges have a wide range of optional dispositions when dealing with adjudicated delinquents. The National Advisory Committee on Criminal Justice Standards and Goals (1976) placed these alternatives into four categories: (1) nominal, (2) conditional, (3) suspended, and (4) custodial dispositions. This section will examine the types of dispositional alternatives available to the juvenile court within each of these categories.

Nominal Dispositions

The best way to understand a nominal disposition is to recognize that at times, the juvenile court, for any number of reasons, will not continue its control and supervision over adjudicated delinquents. It is possible, for example, that a child adjudicated delinquent is given a verbal reprimand by the judge and admonished not to commit further delinquent acts. But because of the relatively minor nature of the present offense or the lack of resources in the juvenile probation office the child is released from community supervision. This approach can be characterized as a passive form of probation.

Conditional Dispositions

As a result of the prominent role played by probation in juvenile court process, conditional dispositions are the most frequent sanctions imposed on adjudicated delinquents. Conditional dispositions involve some form of continuing community supervision and a series of conditions that must be met in order to remain on what is considered "privileged" status. These dispositions may include any or all of the following (Rogers and Mays 1987:425–26):

1. *financial conditions*—these may include fines and restitution. Many juvenile court judges are reluctant to impose fines knowing of most juveniles' inability to pay and the burden placed on some families when fines are ordered. Restitution, however, has become a fairly common condition attached to probation, especially in cases involving theft or damage to property.

2. *community service*—another condition frequently imposed, particularly in the case of relatively minor offenses (such as acts of vandalism), is the completion of a certain number of hours of community service. This service often includes cleaning up city parks and recreational facilities, working at animal shelters, or assisting in hospitals and clinics. One of the chief disadvantages in imposing community service as a conditional disposition is that someone, often the juvenile probation officers, must monitor performance of these services, and this creates an additional burden on an already overburdened probation staff.

3. *remedial services*—these include receiving assistance to correct educational deficiencies, substance abuse treatment, and individual and family counseling. These services usually are provided by community-based organizations.

4. *alternative residential placements*—in situations where a juvenile cannot or should not be left in the home, alternative housing arrangements must be made. These placements may include foster homes, group homes or shelters, and halfway houses.

In most instances, conditional dispositions are administered under the umbrella of the juvenile probation office. When judges place juveniles on probation, they attach a series of conditions to the probation order. This does not mean that juvenile probation officers directly deliver the needed services, but it does mean that they must act as service brokers. For instance, they may frequently assist clients in finding appropriate service delivery agencies.

Suspended Dispositions

Suspended dispositions, much like nominal dispositions, may involve the threat of court action, more than the action itself. In these cases, the judge may be willing to withhold adjudication or imposition of a disposition if the juvenile is willing to demonstrate, or refrain from, certain types of behavior. This is most likely to occur with first offenders or with minor property offenders. Occasionally, when juvenile courts have jurisdiction over traffic offenses, judges will withhold fines or other sanctions if a juvenile does not receive another citation within a specified period of time (frequently six months to a year). A situation like this would best illustrate a suspended disposition.

Custodial Dispositions

Custodial dispositions involve some period of detention or incarceration. These dispositional alternatives normally are imposed as a last resort by juvenile court judges. As a result of the pervasiveness of the regenerative or rehabilitative philosophy in juvenile courts, most judges and juvenile probation officers will try traditional probation or alternatives to incarceration as many times as possible.

Incarceration, therefore, is reserved most frequently for serious (violent) and persistent offenders.

Juveniles can be incarcerated in a variety of correctional facilities (Finckenauer 1984). These facilities range from local, minimum security institutions to traditional, state training schools for both male and female delinquents. The length of time for which a youngster will be incarcerated is determined, in part, by state juvenile statutes and also by juvenile court judges' interpretations and applications of those statutes.

Juvenile courts historically have employed a system of *indeterminate sentencing*. Under this approach, juveniles were sent to correctional facilities for a time period to be determined by correctional authorities. A juvenile's release date, therefore, would be set once he or she was "rehabilitated." This meant that sentences could range from a few weeks to years, when the juvenile might reach the age of majority.

Recently, many states have shifted from indeterminate to determinate sentencing schemes (Bartollas 1990:16; Schneider 1984b). This change in sentencing philosophy means that open-ended sentences have been replaced by commitments of fixed duration. This change in sentencing procedures parallels many of the other changes in juvenile courts, and signals more adultlike treatment of juvenile offenders.

Not only have sentencing procedures changed, but the populations of juvenile correctional facilities have changed as well. As a result of the diversion movement and the deinstitutionalization of status offenders (DSO), (discussed in Chapter 1), training schools house few, if any, status offenders and proportionately more serious offenders. Combined, these two changes demonstrate the "get tough" approach increasingly taken toward serious juvenile offenders.

SERIOUS OFFENDERS AND JUVENILE COURT PUNISHMENTS

By definition, serious offenders are those who merit the most serious punishment. It should be recognized, however, that most states do not have sufficient correctional resources even to house the most serious juvenile offenders. This situation requires states to place some serious offenders on probation. However, based on their violence or offense persistence, serious offenders are more likely to be incarcerated (Speirs 1989). It should be remembered, however, that even with incarceration decisions, there are at least two options for dealing with delinquents.

First, judges can retain serious offenders in the juvenile justice system in an effort to help resolve their problems. The implication of this type of decision is that juveniles, for the most part, are treatable or "redeemable" and should be considered children as long as possible. One result is that some serious offenders pass through the juvenile justice system more than once, and some are incarcerated on multiple occasions. When this happens, juvenile authorities often consider other options for dealing with serious offenders.

The second approach, then, for dealing with serious juvenile offenders is to remove them from juvenile court jurisdiction and send them into the criminal justice system for adjudication. Essentially, waiver of jurisdiction over juvenile offenders implies that: (1) the juvenile justice system does not have the facilities and programs to treat serious offenders, or (2) the youngster's behavior warrants harsher treatment than is available in the juvenile justice system. Both of these justifications will be explored in Chapter 3.

PUBLIC POLICY AND DETERRENCE OF DELINQUENCY

It appears that controlling juvenile crime is a major policy concern for most citizens in the United States as well as for policy makers at all levels of government. This is evidenced by both the quantity of new laws aimed at juvenile offenders and the punitiveness of many of these laws. This section will highlight a few of the major pieces of national legislation and several state policy initiatives of the past three decades.

Federal Legislation

Modern juvenile justice legislation can be traced to the President's Commission on Law Enforcement and the Administration of Justice (1967). This Commission's influential report, *The Challenge of Crime in a Free Society*, clearly expressed the nation's concern with crime generally, and especially with juvenile crime. The Commission's report noted, for example, that "America's best hope for reducing crime is to reduce juvenile delinquency and youth crime" (President's Commission on Law Enforcement and the Administration of Justice 1967:55). As part of the President's Commission there was a Task Force on Juvenile Delinquency. This Task Force in its report *Juvenile Delinquency and Youth Crime* (1967) focused much of its attention on delinquency prevention (especially in such areas as the family, schools, and economics) and system reforms generally aimed at making juvenile justice less stigmatizing and punitive. However, the policy goals were painted in very broad strokes, not specific details.

The thrust of legislation from the Commission's work, however, was aimed at adult crime. The Omnibus Crime Control and Safe Streets Act of 1968 initiated the "war on crime," but most of the "enemy forces" were adult criminals. Juveniles, for the most part, were recognized as contributing to the overall crime statistics, but legislation aimed at delinquent offenders took a long time to evolve.

The Juvenile Justice and Delinquency Prevention Act of 1974, the first major piece of juvenile justice legislation following the work of the President's Commission, has set the tone for dealing with juvenile offenders (Schwartz 1989). Close on the heels of the Juvenile Justice and Delinquency Prevention Act, the National Advisory Committee on Criminal Justice Standards and Goals issued its report entitled *Juvenile Justice and Delinquency Prevention* (1976). Interestingly, like the President's Commission earlier, many of the National Advisory Committee's recommendations were aimed at making the juvenile justice system less punitive. Major policy initiatives included diversion, deinstitutionalization, and decriminalization (Schneider 1984a, 1985). The main philosophical and theoretical underpinnings of the Juvenile Justice and Delinquency Prevention Act were labeling theory and the attendant stigmatization believed to accompany formal processing and adjudication. The result of this trend was removal from the juvenile justice system of large numbers of status and minor delinquent offenders. This left a group of "hardcore" delinquents in the juvenile justice system, and it also made their particular degrees of delinquency more conspicuous. Once the nature and degree of serious delinquency became apparent, the general public urged lawmakers to do something about the new "juvenile crime wave."

The Juvenile Justice and Delinquency Prevention Act of 1974 has since been amended several times. One of the main legislative priorities has been the removal of juveniles from adult jails in most, if not all, circumstances (Schwartz 1989). This initiative has been backed by the power of the federal courts. States are required to monitor the rates of juvenile detention in adult jails and report this information to the Office of Juvenile Justice and Delinquency Prevention. Many types of federal juvenile justice funding are tied to the degree to which juvenile detainees have been kept out of adult facilities.

State Legislation

It would be impossible to discuss all of the state legislative changes since the late 1960s that have impacted on juvenile justice processes. In some ways it is even difficult to summarize those changes. Nevertheless, this section will discuss three important state legislative initiatives.

One of the major changes in state legislation has been a redefinition of delinquency. This redefinition typically, has narrowed the scope of delinquency jurisdiction by delineating status offenders as children in need of supervision (CHINS), or some similar designation indicating that they are not delinquents. Some states have gone even further. For example, Schneider (1984a) notes that the states of Maine and Washington have moved toward total divestiture of juvenile court jurisdiction over status offenders. The upshot of this movement is that juvenile courts are normally left to deal with a smaller caseload of the most serious delinquents, those who have committed what would be serious misdemeanors or felonies if committed by adults. (Feld 1987b; Szymanski 1989).

The second legislative thrust has been in the area of redefining the juvenile court's jurisdiction. This has resulted in lowering the court's maximum age of jurisdiction, lowering the minimum age of transfer, broadening the criteria for transfer, or excluding some offenses from juvenile court consideration altogether.

The third area of legislative development influencing the juvenile justice system is the movement toward greater centralization of agencies, processes, and policies. A number of states (New Mexico is one of the most recent) have adopted the model developed by the California Youth Authority. The result is a conscious effort to minimize much of the fragmentation which has characterized juvenile justice operations in many states. Thus, juvenile probation offices, secure correctional facilities, and parole services are brought under one umbrella, sometimes with agencies providing a variety of other social services to juveniles. Such a policy gives greater consistency across jurisdictions at the cost of loss of local agency autonomy.

These legislative changes, combined with many others, have resulted in altering the basic nature of the juvenile justice system without eliminating it altogether. In fact, most jurisdictions have adapted to these changes while keeping juvenile justice a viable entity.

SUMMARY

The concept of juvenile justice is one with many precursors, but the most advanced development of what can be called a juvenile justice system has been in the United States. A system for dealing with juvenile offenders separate and apart from adults can be traced back to the mid-1800s, with the end of the Civil War, the beginning of the Industrial Revolution, a period of great immigration from Europe and the Orient, and the influence of the Progressive movement. All of these factors contributed to the creation of the first juvenile court in 1899, and this court proved to be the cornerstone upon which the juvenile justice system would be built.

For most of the twentieth century, the treatment of juveniles as a separate and distinct category of offenders was intended to be informal, confidential, nonstigmatizing, regenerative, and benevolent. The reality, however, was that in return for these potential benefits, juveniles received few legal rights and protections. However, in the 1960s, when constitutional due process rights were expanded dramatically for adults, the issue of procedural due process for accused juvenile offenders became more prominent. With adult cases such as *Gideon* and *Miranda*, the relatively disadvantaged status of all criminal offenders became apparent, and when juvenile court procedures were measured against these standards, the discrepancies became even more dramatic. Consequently, for a period of six or seven years (starting in 1966) a whole new set of constitutional rights was articulated for accused delinquents by the United States Supreme Court and other federal and state appellate courts.

With the "due process revolution" in juvenile procedures came attendant costs, however. Many policy makers felt that if juveniles were going to receive adultlike protections, they should be exposed to adultlike sanctions (see Regnery 1989). The result has been increasingly punitive procedures aimed at serious, violent, and persistent youthful offenders.

Before jumping to the conclusion that juvenile procedures have become more adultlike for all offenders, however, it is important to note that the juvenile justice system is becoming more punitive and less punitive at the same time. While more stringent measures like mandatory or determinate sentences and additional transfers to adult courts have been witnessed, some juveniles are sanctioned less frequently and less severely by juvenile courts. Less severe treatment has been experienced especially by status offenders—many of whom were treated as delinquents prior to 1974—and minor property offenders.

A number of states have limited the capacity of their juvenile correctional facilities, or have been financially unable to expand them, causing institutional bed space to be reserved for the most serious or persistent offenders. A few states (e.g., Florida and Massachusetts) have actually reduced the number of bed spaces available for adjudicated offenders (see, e.g., Bartollas 1990; Pingree 1984). The result has been fairly large-scale diversion of juvenile offenders from the formal adjudicative process into community-based treatment programs. Even many adjudicated delinquents are placed in alternatives to incarceration because of lack of space or lack of funds.

In terms of this brief overview of the juvenile justice system, several summary points can be made. First, juvenile justice procedures no longer resemble those envisioned by the founders of our first juvenile courts. Juvenile records often are no longer confidential (since some states allow routine publication of juvenile suspects' names); informal (since rules of procedure must be applied); or nonadversarial (since attorneys are present in many cases, and some states provide for a nonwaivable right to counsel by juvenile suspects). Ironically, though, the philosophical foundations—parens patriae treatment and rehabilitation—persist as integral features of the juvenile justice system (see Cullen et al. 1983). The outcome has been a confusing, or contradictory approach to meting out justice to juveniles. It is as if we have tried to put new wine into old wine skins; the old philosophies cannot accommodate the new procedures for long.

NOTE

1. Davis (1980:12) notes that thirteen states provide for juvenile jury trials either by statutes or court decision. These states include: Alaska, Colorado, Kansas, Massachusetts, Michigan, Montana, New Mexico, Oklahoma, South Dakota, Texas, West Virginia, Wisconsin, and Wyoming. Rubin (1984:116) adds Illinois to this list in cases involving habitual juvenile offenders.

CHAPTER 3

Transfer Hearings: State Variations

Chapter 2 provided a brief overview of the juvenile justice system, and one of the key points concerning the evolution of that system is the way juvenile offenders, especially serious offenders, have been viewed. In general, punishments for delinquent offenders have become increasingly severe during the 1980s. Indicators of this punitiveness include the increasing numbers and types of offenders considered for transfer from juvenile court to adult criminal court.

This chapter will consider the nature, processes, and justifications for treating alleged delinquents as adults. However, some basic points need to be made explicit before our overview continues. First, transfer provisions have been a part of many states' juvenile codes for decades. In simplest terms, this means that we are not dealing with a new phenomenon. Second, until the late 1960s, relatively few children were transferred, and very little attention was given to transfer provisions. Recently this aspect of juvenile court procedure has received increased emphasis and visibility (Feld 1987b). Third, in reality there have never been great numbers of juveniles tried as adults, although such occurrences are important symbolically, if not practically.

Finally, if recent trends in juvenile procedures continue, one of two scenarios is likely to take place. Either (1) it will be difficult to justify juvenile courts as separate entities, or (2) increasing numbers of juveniles identified as "serious" offenders will be sent to the criminal justice system for adjudication.

TRANSFERS, CERTIFICATIONS, AND WAIVERS

A variety of terms are used to describe the processing of juveniles as adults. Although the most commonly used are *transfers* and *waivers of jurisdiction*, some state juvenile codes also include the terms *certification* or *remands* (Gillespie and Norman 1984; Snyder 1987). A comparison of various juvenile codes reveals virtually no difference in the meaning of these terms, and in their use in this chapter, no difference in meaning is implied.

The idea of providing a transfer mechanism is that there may be circumstances under which it would be more appropriate (or desirable) to adjudicate a juvenile using adult criminal court processes rather than juvenile court procedures (see, e.g., Speirs 1989). The following sections will elaborate on the purposes, bases, and goals of transfers.

Purposes of Transfers

The transfer of accused delinquents to adult court is an exceptional occurrence by definition (Bortner 1986; Feld 1987b; Snyder 1987). Snyder et al. (1985) note that of the 10,000 juvenile petitions they reviewed, two percent resulted in waivers.

One of the manifest assumptions of juvenile procedures traditionally has been that children, all children, are worth redeeming (Price 1990). The President's Commission on Law Enforcement and Administration of Justice (1967:79) said, for example, that juvenile courts "differ from adult criminal courts in a number of basic respects, reflecting the philosophy that children should be protected and rehabilitated rather than subjected to the harshness of the criminal system." In some ways this is the reason for the very existence of the juvenile justice system. Therefore, only under the most extreme circumstances have juveniles been considered for transfer to adult courts. These decisions have been reached in one of two circumstances.

Waivers of justification have been viewed as appropriate in the case of children who have committed particularly violent, personal offenses. The National Advisory Committee for Juvenile Justice and Delinquency Prevention (1980) characterizes these offenses as heinous or aggravated in nature. For example, in the State of New Mexico, juveniles over the age of fifteen can be tried as adults for homicide (New Mexico Statutes Annotated, Section 32–1–30). In such cases it may make little difference whether and to what extent a juvenile has a record of arrests and delinquency adjudications. One very serious offense is sufficient to convince some juvenile judges that a youngster deserves to face the full penalty of the criminal law, rather than the solicitous, protective atmosphere of the juvenile court.

The second type of children likely to be certified to stand trial as adults are older juvenile offenders (especially sixteen- and seventeen-year-olds) who have an extensive offense history, particularly for property offenses (Nimick et al. 1986). These youngsters frequently have lengthy records of arrests, diversions, adjudications, probation, and even incarceration. In other words, many of them have lengthy records of recidivism within the juvenile justice system. The assumption often made by the juvenile judge and the probation staff is that there is little, if anything, to offer such a child in the juvenile justice system. Treatment programs do not seem effective, or the adolescent is determined not to respond to treatment efforts. In such cases, remand to the adult courts seems logical and reasonable.

Bases for Transfer

The legal precedents for transfer decisions in most jurisdictions have been profoundly influenced by *Kent v. United States*, (1966) discussed briefly in Chapter 2. In this section, we will look in greater detail at the due process provisions mandated by *Kent* and some of the legislative provisions based on that case.

Throughout much of the juvenile court's history, judges were those solely authorized to decide whether to transfer juveniles to adult court jurisdiction (Feld 1987b). This approach left juvenile judges with virtually unlimited discretion in waiving jurisdiction over youths and remanding them to adult courts. However, *Kent v. United States* changed juvenile court operations considerably.

In *Kent*, a sixteen-year-old youth from Washington, D.C. was accused of burglary, robbery, and rape. The juvenile court judge decided, without a full hearing on the issues, that the facts of the case warranted trying Kent as an adult. On appeal, Kent's attorney focused on three issues: (1) the right to counsel during transfer decision making processes, (2) the right to a full hearing on the transfer issue and justifications for the transfer, and (3) access to the court's social records by the juvenile's attorney.

In its opinion in *Kent v. United States*, the Supreme Court noted that there were several factors juvenile court judges should assess in making the transfer decision. These factors were

1. The seriousness of the alleged offense to the community and whether the protection of the community requires waiver;
2. Whether the alleged offense was committed in an aggressive, violent, premeditated or willful manner;
3. Whether the alleged offense was against persons or against property, greater weight being given to offenses against persons especially if personal injury resulted;
4. The prosecutive merit of the complaint, i.e., whether there is evidence upon which a grand jury may be expected to return an indictment;
5. The desirability of trial and disposition of the entire offense in one court when the juvenile's associates in the alleged offense are adults;
6. The sophistication and maturity of the juvenile by consideration of his home, environmental situation, emotional attitude, and pattern of living;
7. The record and previous history of the juvenile, including previous contacts with . . . law enforcement agencies, juvenile courts and other jurisdictions, prior periods of probation . . . or prior commitments to juvenile institutions;
8. The prospects for adequate protection of the public and the likelihood of reasonable rehabilitation of the juvenile (if he is found to have committed the alleged offense) by the use of procedures, services, and facilities currently available to the juvenile court.

Many states have incorporated these provisions into their juvenile codes, in some instances, verbatim. A review of the eight factors outlined by the Supreme Court in *Kent* reveals that they can be divided into two broad classifications. These two categories—danger to the public and amenability to treatment—are now parts of many state juvenile codes, and while both are fairly self-explanatory each remains controversial in its own way.

Dangerousness to the public presents a problem to juvenile justice decision makers. It is a prediction of future actions, which is normally extrapolated from past behavior. However, what should be done about the youngster who commits a homicide but has no previous record of delinquency? What are the most appropriate bases for predicting future behavior? What are the most accurate predictors?

The answers to these questions, unfortunately, require clinical diagnoses not only beyond the capabilities of a judge, but frequently unavailable to juvenile court judges. In fact, Feld (1981:500) says that one of the essential problems is "Judges rely on clinical evaluations to determine a youth's . . . dangerousness—a reliance that raises questions about the validity of clinical diagnoses or predictions and the propriety of delegating issues of social policy to the discretionary judgments of social service personnel and judges."

The second category—amenability to treatment—seems equally illusive (Bortner 1986:58–59; Davis 1980:15; Grisso 1981:21). Amenability is often measured negatively, that is, by lack of responsiveness to treatment. While this may be easier to demonstrate empirically than dangerousness, it is still problematic.

Lack of amenability to treatment means, in simplest terms, that some type of treatment or intervention program has been attempted before with this youngster, but to no avail (Binder 1979:649). Perhaps some juveniles have passed through the system a number of times— through previous correctional commitments. Obviously nothing has worked, because they are back again for new offenses. The point often overlooked when considering this justification for transfer is if there is "fault"—it may be attributable to the child, the family, the juvenile justice system itself, or any combination of the three. This point will be explored further in the section pertaining to who gets transferred.

Goals of Transfers

Perhaps the best way to compare the possible goals of transfers would be to recite the normal purposes of sentencing (Bortner 1986;

Feld 1987b). Some view the varying purposes of sanctioning to be mutually exclusive, but that is not necessarily the case.

Retribution, one of the oldest purposes of criminal sentencing, actually predates formalized systems of sanctions. Retribution is punishment, but commensurate with the offense committed and the amount of punishment deserved (Bortner 1988). Most correctional researchers date this philosophy to the formation of the *lex talionis*, or law of retribution expressed in such early documents as the Mosaic law and the Code of Hammurabi (Drowns and Hess 1990). In theory, retribution should be one of the primary justifications for transferring juveniles to adult courts. Such a move should provide punishment commensurate with the commission of serious offenses.

Isolation or incapacitation is another sentencing philosophy. Incapacitation assumes that incarcerating an offender will curb law-violating behavior. Again, in theory, incapacitation should result from the certification of juvenile offenders to stand trial as adults (assuming, of course, that they are eventually convicted). Waiver of juvenile court jurisdiction should permit the incarceration of convicted offenders in more secure settings (e.g., adult prisons) and for longer periods of time than are legally permissible in the juvenile justice system.

Rehabilitation has been the prevailing sentencing philosophy for the juvenile courts since their inception (see Armstrong and Altschuler 1982; Bortner 1986; Braithwaite and Shore 1981; Weisheit and Alexander 1988). Retention of jurisdiction over juvenile offenders reaffirms the rehabilitative philosophy. Thus, waiver of jurisdiction appears to be a repudiation of that doctrine. Therefore, it appears that rehabilitation is the sanctioning justification least compatible with waivers of jurisdiction.

Deterrence has become one of the primary sentencing justifications since the partial, or total repudiation of the rehabilitation philosophy (Feld 1984b). Deterrence presumes that punishing an offender will prevent him or her from committing further acts of deviance (specific deterrence), or will dissuade others from law-violating behavior (general deterrence). There is much debate about whether or not increasing severity of punishment deters offenders, but in theory, the transfer of juveniles to adult court should serve a deterrent function.

No matter which sanctioning philosophies guide waiver of jurisdiction over juvenile offenders—two things are apparent. First, juveniles are transferred because seemingly, they cannot be punished harshly enough in the juvenile justice system, or second, they are transferred because treatment services are insufficient in the juvenile justice system. However, it is equally possible that neither or both of these factors plays an explicit role in transfer decision making.

TRANSFER HEARINGS

Transfer hearings are conducted to determine whether the juvenile court should waive jurisdiction and remand the juvenile to the adult criminal courts. However, before continuing it is important to examine the age factors associated with transfers.

Two ages are of particular importance when considering the transfer issue: (1) the maximum age of juvenile court jurisdiction, and (2) the minimum age at which a juvenile can be tried as an adult. As Table 3.1 shows, most states use eighteen as the maximum age for juvenile offenders. In fact, thirty-nine states and the District of Columbia utilize eighteen years of age as the upper age limit for juvenile court jurisdiction. Ten states have age limits below eighteen, and one state (Wyoming) uses nineteen years as the juvenile court's maximum jurisdictional age.

Although the juvenile court's maximum age limit is important, the focus of this book is on the age at which a juvenile can be transferred to adult court. Table 3.2 lists the youngest age at which a state can remand a youngster to an adult criminal court (see also Szymanski 1989). It should be noted however, that some states utilize multiple age classification categories, depending on the offense with which the youth is charged.[1]

Another crucial legal factor related to waiver decisions is the amount of evidence necessary to justify a waiver. The National Advisory Committee for Juvenile Justice and Delinquency Prevention (1980) recommended that "clear and convincing evidence" must exist that the child is not amenable to treatment, in order to justify a waiver decision. Currently, there seems to be a great deal of variation regarding the amount of evidence necessary and the party bearing the burden of proof, in transfer hearings. As an illustration, the evidence required may be by "fair preponderance of the evidence" (as in Alaska); by "clear and convincing evidence" (as in

Table 3.1
Age at which criminal courts gain jurisdiction over young offenders

Age of offender when under criminal court jurisdiction	States
16	Connecticut, New York, North Carolina
17	Georgia, Illinois, Louisiana, Massachusetts, Missouri, South Carolina, Texas
18	Alabama, Alaska, Arizona, Arkansas, California, Colorado, Delaware, District of Columbia, Florida, Hawaii, Idaho, Indiana, Iowa, Kansas, Kentucky, Maine, Maryland, Michigan, Minnesota, Mississippi, Montana, Nebraska, Nevada, New Hampshire, New Jersey, New Mexico, North Dakota, Ohio, Oklahoma, Oregon, Pennsylvania, Rhode Island, South Dakota, Tennessee, Utah, Vermont, Virginia, Washington, West Virginia, Wisconsin, federal districts
19	Wyoming

Source: Bureau of Justice Statistics, Report to the Nation on Crime and Justice, 2d ed. Washington, DC: U.S. Department of Justice, 1988.

Massachusetts); by the "preponderance of the evidence" (in states like Nevada and Washington); or by "substantial evidence" (in Kansas and Oklahoma) ("Certification—Burden of Proof: Alaska," 1987; see also Court Decisions 1985). Additionally, while most juvenile codes place the burden of proof for certification on the state, California requires juveniles charged with certain serious offenses to prove that they are amenable to treatment and therefore should not be remanded to the adult criminal courts. Therefore, although *Kent v.*

Table 3.2
Judicial waiver ages by state

Youngest age at which juvenile may be transferred to criminal court by judicial waiver	States
No specific age	Alaska, Arizona, Arkansas, Delaware, Florida, Indiana, Kentucky, Maine, Maryland, New Hampshire, New Jersey, Oklahoma, South Dakota, West Virginia, Wyoming, federal districts
10	Vermont
12	Montana
13	Georgia, Illinois, Mississippi
14	Alabama, Colorado, Connecticut, Idaho, Iowa, Massachusetts, Minnesota, Missouri, North Carolina, North Dakota, Pennsylvania, South Carolina, Tennessee, Utah
15	District of Columbia, Louisiana, Michigan, New Mexico, Ohio, Oregon, Texas, Virginia
16	California, Hawaii, Kansas, Nevada, Rhode Island, Washington, Wisconsin

Source: Bureau of Justice Statistics, Report to the Nation on Crime and Justice, 2d ed. Washington, DC : U.S. Department of Justice, 1988.

United States (and similar cases) outlined the general due process requirements for waivers, individual states still retain a great deal of autonomy in determining the final nature of the protections extended.

Now that we have considered the purposes of transfer hearings and the statutory age parameters imposed on juvenile courts, the

following section will examine three methods, or systems by which transfers are made.

Judicial Waivers

The primary method whereby juvenile courts traditionally have made transfer decisions has been the judicial waiver (Nimick et al. 1986). Presently, forty-eight states still provide for some form of this process (U.S. Department of Justice 1988b). In simplest terms, this means that the judge is the primary, if not the exclusive decision maker in the transfer process. If the state files a motion with the court to have the youth tried as an adult, the court must consider the evidence presented in the transfer hearing and decide whether the transfer is in the best interests of the child as well as the public.

Judicial waiver processes, for the most part, remained unchallenged until the *Kent* case in 1966. In *Kent* one of the chief constitutional challenges was the sufficiency of the waiver hearing. A quick reading of the *Kent* decision reveals that the juvenile court judge, in the District of Columbia, gave only a cursory review of Kent's case, and in the absence of an attorney, remanded Kent to adult court jurisdiction. In responding to Kent's appeal, the United States Supreme Court noted that representation by an attorney was an essential element of procedural due process, and that a full examination of the facts surrounding the case—in other words, a transfer hearing— was necessary to adequately determine whether to try the juvenile as an adult.

The eight factors articulated in *Kent*, discussed previously in this chapter, were designed to give guidance to juvenile court judges in deciding whether to waive jurisdiction over certain juvenile offenders. Therefore, based on *Kent* and cases that followed, the appellate courts consistently have held that judges do not have absolute discretion in making waiver decisions. In fact, many states have incorporated the *Kent* standards into their juvenile codes. Thus, we may say that judges have had certain limits imposed on them in the process of waiver decision making.

Table 3.3 lists some of the most common reasons juveniles are transferred to criminal courts for trial. While not all statutory justifications are included in this table, the most common offenses included in state juvenile codes are listed (see also Szymanski 1989).

Table 3.3
Reasons for waiving juveniles to adult courts, based on present offense

Current Offenses	States[1]
Murder[2]	California, Delaware, Georgia, Indiana, Kentucky, Maine, Minnesota, New Jersey, New Mexico, South Carolina, Virginia, West Virginia
Robbery or armed robbery	California, Delaware, Georgia, New Jersey, West Virginia
Kidnapping	California, Georgia, Minnesota, New Jersey, West Virginia
Rape	California, Delaware, Georgia, Minnesota, New Jersey, New Mexico, South Carolina, Virginia, West Virginia
Burglary or aggravated burglary	Georgia, Minnesota, New Mexico, South Carolina
Aggravated assault	South Carolina
Other[3]	Connecticut, Florida, Georgia, Hawaii, Indiana, Kentucky, Maine, Maryland, Massachusetts, Minnesota, New Jersey, North Carolina, Virginia, West Virginia

Source: Barry C. Feld, "The Juvenile Court Meets the Principle of the Offense: Legislative Changes in Juvenile Waiver Statutes." Reprinted by special permission of Northwestern University, School of Law, Volume 78:3, Journal of Criminal Law & Criminology, pages 505-8 (1987).

1 Not all states specify particular offenses serving as the basis for waiver desisions (i.e., some statutes prescribe "any" offense or "felonies" as justifying waivers). Some states are inclided in this list more than once since they stipulate a number of offenses eligible for waiver.

2 In some states (e.g., Georgia, Kentucky, Maryland, and North Carolina) the specification is for "capital" offenses.

3 This category includes offenses such as "class A, B, or C felonies;" "personal violence;" "aggravated felonies;" or simply "felonies."

Legislative Waivers

In some ways, legislative waivers are not really waivers at all. Rather, they are constraints imposed on the juvenile court's jurisdiction by the legislature (Feld 1984b). These limits generally arise within a fairly narrow range of cases. For example, some states do not allow juvenile courts to have jurisdiction over traffic offenses (Law Enforcement Assistance Administration 1980). These cases are heard in the same courts as adult traffic cases, typically, courts of inferior jurisdiction such as municipal or magistrate's courts.

At the most serious end of the continuum, however, legislatures have increasingly imposed limits on juvenile court jurisdiction over youngsters who have committed the most severe felonies (i.e., those cases calling for life imprisonment or the death penalty, if committed by adults). The assumption in these cases is that juvenile courts cannot impose sufficiently stringent penalties; thus, adult courts should have jurisdiction over these cases. Speirs (1989:4) says "Many assume that for similar offenses adults receive more severe dispositions in criminal court than juveniles do in juvenile court." Davis (1980:17) concludes that one reason legislatures exclude offenses from a court's jurisdiction is to demonstrate "that the community may be outraged at the commission of the more serious offenses, whether the offender is an adult or a child, and it may feel the need to express its social and moral condemnation through the harsh medium of the criminal process."

Through the use of limits imposed on juvenile court jurisdiction, legislatures have played an increasingly important role in juvenile procedures. Legislatures have given expression to the more punitive attitudes held by many members of the general public and public policy makers. In fact, legislatures have contributed to more adultlike atmospheres in juvenile justice settings, and the blurring of distinctions between juvenile and adult courts. Table 3.4 lists some of the offenses state legislatures have excluded from juvenile court jurisdictions.

Prosecutorial Waivers

Perhaps the most controversial waiver system is that involving prosecutorial initiative. In a small group of states (Florida and Utah,

Table 3.4
Offenses excluded from juvenile court jurisdictions

Excluded Offenses	States[1]
Murder[2]	Arkansas, Connecticut, Delaware, District of Columbia, Idaho, Illinois, Indiana, Louisiana, Nevada, New York, Ohio, Oklahoma, Pennsylvania Utah, Vermont
Rape (including criminal sexual conduct or penetration)	Arkansas, Delaware, District of Columbia, Idaho, Illinois Indiana, Louisiana, New York Oklahoma, Utah, Vermont
Kidnapping	Delaware, Indiana, Louisiana New York, Oklahoma, Utah
Burglary	District of Columbia, Louisiana, New York
Armed robbery or robbery	District of Columbia, Idaho, Illinois, Indiana, Louisiana, Maryland, Oklahoma, Utah, Vermont
Other[3]	Arkansas, Colorado, Connecticut, Florida, Idaho, Kansas, Nebraska, Ohio, Rhode Island, Wyoming

Source: Barry C. Feld, "The Juvenile Court Meets the Principle of the Offense: Legislative Changes in Juvenile Waiver Statutes." Reprinted by special permission of Northwestern University, School of Law, Volume 78:3, Journal of Criminal Law & Criminology, pages 512-14 (1987).

[1] Only 23 states plus the District of Columbia legislatively exclude certain offenses from juvenile court jurisdiction. Because of the different offense categories, some states are listed more than once.

[2] This category includes various degrees of criminal homicide including attempted murder in some states (e. g., Nevada and New York).

[3] This category includes offense categories such as "any offense" may be excluded; "Class I, II, and III" offenses; "mayhem;" "arson;" "felony 1, 2 ;" and "manslaughter."

for example), the prosecuting attorney has the authority under state law to decide in which court to file a case (Davis 1980:17ff; Gillespie and Norman 1984; Note 1982; Thomas and Bilchik 1985). This discretion is based on juvenile courts and criminal courts having concurrent jurisdiction over most cases, and it allows the prosecutor to bypass juvenile courts altogether in certain cases, and to directly file criminal charges in adult courts. This procedure, like others discussed previously, is another indicator of the increasing degree of punitiveness in the juvenile justice system.

Prosecutorial waivers, however, are not without controversy. For one thing, there is the issue of the prosecutor's dominance of the entire juvenile court intake process (see, e.g., Note 1982; Rubin 1980). Bortner (1986:65) says that in prosecutorial waiver states

the highly political nature of the office is reflected in the stress the prosecutor places upon public outcry for more punitive sanctioning of juveniles. The prosecutor also exercises the greatest discretion regarding remand decisions. The most political actor in the juvenile court setting has the greatest power to respond to perceived public demand for remand.

There is also a legal question concerning the exercise of discretion by the prosecutors without counterbalancing accountability. In other words, when judges make decisions about waiving jurisdiction over juvenile offenders, those decisions are appealable. When prosecutors exercise their discretion in the transfer process, those decisions are practically without administrative or judicial review (see, e.g., *People v. Portland* 1979; *People v. Thorpe* 1982). Interestingly, appellate courts have held that prosecutors traditionally have exercised degrees and types of discretion not permissible for judges. Thus, prosecutors enjoy vast amounts of unchecked decision-making authority and may play an ever-increasing role in shaping the juvenile court's future.

AUTOMATIC TRANSFERS

Automatic transfer provisions are best understood in relation to legislative waiver provisions discussed in the previous section. In this section we will examine the purposes for automatically waiving juveniles to adult criminal courts. Before going further, however, it should be noted that not all states employ these provisions, and where they are utilized most automatic waivers involve offenses calling for the death penalty or life imprisonment (Law Enforcement Assistance Administration 1980:50).

In most instances, states utilize automatic waivers in cases of the most serious or persistent offenders. For these youths, the legislature may provide that—if a child commits certain types of offenses (e.g., homicide, rape, or robbery); the child has been charged with a certain number of serious (felony) offenses; or the child has a certain number of previous delinquency adjudications—the juvenile court loses jurisdiction and the case will go through the ordinary process of criminal adjudication (Law Enforcement Assistance Administration 1980). For example, in *State v. Bernard* (1979), the Rhode Island Supreme Court upheld the state's automatic waiver of a juvenile who had twice been found delinquent after the age of sixteen. The court held that the legislature had the authority to exclude certain offenders from juvenile court jurisdiction. In fact, "the Legislature had the power to remove *all* juveniles over fifteen from the jurisdiction of the juvenile court" ("Transfer/Due Process/Equal Protection: Rhode Island" 1979). The view held by most appellate courts is that jurisdiction is legislatively created and it can be legislatively eliminated through provisions such as automatic transfers. This means that there has been no articulation of a constitutional "right" to be adjudicated as a juvenile.

Automatic waivers are predicated on the assumption that some offenders are not fit for the juvenile court's solicitous, regenerative care. This seems particularly true for violent personal offenders and, as Nimick et al. (1986:2) point out in their study "Cases referred for an index violent offense were the most likely to be waived." These youngsters have demonstrated by their actions that they deserve the levels of punishment or incapacitation associated with the adult criminal justice system. However, as with many decisions made in the criminal justice system, we must not assume that automatic waiver provisions exclude discretion in the process. Indeed, it is possible that the judge or the prosecutor could avoid an automatic waiver simply by ignoring the juvenile's prior record. It is also possible that the court could conduct a transfer hearing and find that the automatic waiver provisions do not apply to the youth because of "extenuating circumstances" (many state juvenile codes have "escape clauses" typically provided under the rubric of "manifest injustice" or some similarly vague provision).

It is safe to say that automatic transfer legislation can provide for more severe punishment for juvenile offenders. However, it is also true that such provisions are largely symbolic. Like the broader picture for waivers themselves, automatic waivers are unlikely to be applied to most juvenile offenders, even the most serious ones. Although automatic waivers remain largely symbolic, they do comport with the retributionist and deterrence philosophies discussed previously.

WHO GETS TRANSFERRED?

It is possible that the juveniles who get remanded to adult court are not the ones most deserving of more serious treatment based on the ostensible purposes of transfers? This section will explore this question in terms of the actual data relating to who gets transferred, rather than in the abstract.

Transferred juveniles might be characterized as the "bad," the "mad," the uncooperative, and those who have nothing else to lose. The "bad" are the dangerous or persistent juvenile offenders. These are the children for whom the transfer process originally was intended: children for whom the juvenile justice system holds little hope for appropriate treatment or improvement. Nimick et al. (1986:3) point out in their study of 2,335 cases waived to criminal court that over one-third (34.3 percent) of the cases involved index violent offenses. Of all cases waived, 6.2 percent were charged with murder, 3.5 percent were charged with rape, 15.5 percent were charged with robbery, and 9 percent were charged with aggravated assault.

The "mad" are delinquents who suffer from various forms of mental illness, but who have come into contact with the juvenile justice system because of violations of the law. These children suffer from two types of problems—delinquency and mental illness. They are, simply, twice deviant. Simonsen and Gordon (1982:122ff) characterize these youths as "defectives," in that something is deficient in their mental or emotional makeup. Often, the choice for the juvenile justice system is whether to treat their mental illness and ignore their delinquency, or to ignore their delinquency and remove them from justice system processes altogether (Simonsen and Gordon 1982:122–33). Unfortunately, few states have the facilities or resources to deal with both of these types of problems at the same time. The solution may be to transfer these youngsters to the adult justice system where treatment services may be available. Some state (Florida, for example) have juvenile code provisions which allow for transfer on demand of the accused delinquent (Carter 1984; Law Enforcement Assistance Administration 1980). In short, the juvenile can petition the court to be transferred into the adult system in hopes of receiving the necessary treatment services.

Uncooperative juveniles are those who have all of the characteristics deemed appropriate for treatment and who, in the estimation of juvenile authorities, would be good candidates for treatment in the juvenile justice system. However, these youths refuse to be treated or to respond to treatment. They should get "better" (i.e., refrain from law-violating behavior), but they do not. As a result of their failure to cooperate with juvenile authorities—judges, juvenile probation officers, and correctional officials—these youths are transferred to the adult system. Such an action often occurs from a sense of frustration, or in order to "teach these kids a lesson."

The juveniles who have nothing to lose are often persistent but minor property offenders. They may look bad compared with other juvenile offenders, but in the adult system, they appear to be rather insignificant transgressors (see, e.g., Sagatun et al. 1985). For them, transfer to adult court and the prospect of a jury trial may result in less serious treatment than they would receive by remaining in the juvenile justice system (see, e.g., Champion 1990; Speirs 1989). In a study of California youths transferred to adult court, Sagatun and her colleagues (1985:86) found that "minors in criminal court were in fact less likely to receive the severest sentence available to the court than were minors in the juvenile court." Feld (1981:513) says that this lenience carries over for some period and "that for about two years following their graduation from juvenile court, young adults are treated more leniently than older offenders."

This treatment may even hold for children who are accused of fairly serious personal crimes, excluding homicide. Adult court judges and juries may view these violations as serious, but the violators are deemed in need of something other than imprisonment. In summarizing who gets transferred, it is worth reiterating a point made earlier. It is possible from the traditional parens patriae view to consider each transfer as evidence of a failure. However, it is important to recognize that the failure may be on the part of the child, the child's family, the juvenile justice system, or all three.

Whatever the source of the dysfunction, it is important to explore the outcomes of transfer procedures. The following section will examine the outcomes for juveniles transferred to adult courts, whether they are the bad, the mad, the uncooperative, or those who have nothing to lose by being tried as adults.

PUBLIC POLICY AND COSMETIC CHANGES: THE EFFECTIVENESS OF TRANSFERS

Four things can be assumed about public policy initiatives, regardless of the substantive area they might address:

1. some policies will be effective and will work as they were envisioned;
2. some policies will work, but not as they were originally intended to work;
3. some policies will not work, even though attempted as originally designed;
4. some policies do not work because they were not implemented as intended.

This section will examine the outcomes of transfer decisions in terms of their effectiveness, based on the ostensible reasons for employing this process. It is possible that transfers are accomplishing what they are intended to, or that they may actually serve as "eyewash" or "whitewash."

To assess the effectiveness of transfers, we must ask: to what extent is public safety being enhanced or the delivery of treatment services being increased? The answers to these questions should tell us something about the general effectiveness of the waiver of jurisdiction process. The logical basis for increasing the frequency with which juveniles are waived to criminal courts is the broader range of punishments that may be imposed. For example, the death penalty is the most severe punishment in a majority of states; however, juvenile court jurisdiction does not include the death penalty as an option. Also, when compared with adult prison terms, the periods of incarceration for juveniles are relatively short.

In terms of sheer numbers, most juveniles transferred to adult courts are property offenders. In fact, in a study by Nimick and her associates (1986) it was found that of 2,335 cases waived to criminal court, 40.3 percent of the juveniles were charged with index property offenses, compared with 34.3 percent charged with index personal offenses and 25.4 percent charged with nonindex offenses (see also Gillespie and Norman 1984; Office of Juvenile Justice and Delinquency Prevention, 1989:53). Because they outnumber violent offenders and tend to be persistent, property offenders are those most likely to be deemed "not amenable to treatment." However, it is important to note that transfer is still a relatively rare occurrence. In fact, Nimick et al. (1986:2) found that about 2 percent of the cases they studied were transferred, and Snyder (1987:46) found that all types of waivers account for only about 5 percent of juvenile court delinquency dispositions.

When juvenile offenders are transferred to adult court, they often do not receive the type of punishment originally intended for them. In fact, transfer does not even necessarily mean that they will be subjected to prosecution. Also, it does not automatically mean that more severe punishments will be meted out by criminal court judges; although this motive is the driving force behind such transfers. While many of these offenders are relatively serious compared with other juveniles appearing before the juvenile court, their offenses are minor in comparison to the perpetrators coming before the adult courts (Bortner 1986:56; Sagatun et al. 1985:88–89). Studies by August (1981) and others (Reed 1983; Sagatun et al. 1985; Schack and Nessen 1984) consistently reflect a high degree of leniency in dealing with those juveniles transferred. If charges are not dismissed or reduced, then the penalties are not as severe, compared with those for adult offenders, crime for crime.

For example, Speirs (1989:4) maintains that when using a "substantial disposition" as the comparison criterion, "juvenile courts intervened in the lives of a greater proportion of violent offenders than did criminal courts." A relatively recent study of the ultimate dispositions of juvenile transfers in selected counties in four southern states for the years 1980–1988 appears to confirm the general findings of others (Champion 1989a). Out of 3,424 transfer hearings during this nine-year period, 2,818 (82 percent) resulted in successful waivers. Proportionately, there were increasing numbers of successful

Table 3.5
Aggregate numbers of waiver hearings and transfers to adult courts in Virginia, Tennessee, Mississippi, and Georgia, 1980–1988

Year	Number of Hearings	Waivers	Percentage
1980	228	163	71.5
1981	249	179	71.9
1982	301	226	75.1
1983	356	294	82.6
1984	451	385	85.3
1985	416	337	81.0
1986	485	419	86.1
1987	472	413	87.6
1988	466	402	86.2
totals	3,424	2,818	82.3

1980 - 1988 increase: 238 cases (104.3%)

Source: Dean J. Champion, "Teenage Felons and Waiver Hearings: Some Recent Trends, 1980 - 1988." Crime and Delinquency, 35 (October 1989), p. 580. Reprinted with permission.

waiver hearings during the 1980–1988 period. However, the percentage of property offenses as subjects of these successful waiver hearings increased over the years from 19 percent to about 50 percent. During the same period, violent crimes accounted for a decreasing part of these successful waiver hearings: from 80 percent in 1980 to 41 percent in 1988. The actual numbers of cases involving violent crimes increased during the same time interval, although proportionate decreases were observed. Tables 3.5, 3.6, and 3.7 show, respectively, the yearly waiver trends, the percentage annual distribution of transfer offenses, and the final annual dispositions.

Additionally, Champion (1990) shows that over 50 percent of the juveniles transferred are placed on probation. This is necessitated by both the comparatively minor nature of the crimes and by an overwhelming lack of adult prison space for all offenders, let alone sixteen- and seventeen-year-old offenders. Therefore, it seems that if we intend to punish juveniles more severely by sending them to

Table 3.6

Offense categories for successful waiver hearings, 1980–1988

Offenses	Year (Percent Rounded to Nearest Whole Number)								
	1980	1981	1982	1983	1984	1985	1986	1987	1988
Homicide	42	39	38	36	35	34	35	32	31
Vehicular theft	6	7	7	8	9	11	15	16	17
Arson	NA	NA	NA	2	3	4	4	3	5
Aggravated Assault	4	5	5	2	2	2	2	5	4
Burglary	4	7	8	16	17	16	14	16	17
Larceny	9	12	14	16	17	20	15	15	16
Robbery	20	17	13	11	8	7	6	5	8
Rape	14	12	11	8	7	4	4	3	3
Other	1	1	4	1	2	2	5	5	3
Total Percent	100	100	100	100	100	100	100	100	100
Number	163	179	226	294	385	337	419	413	402

Grand Total = 2,818 waivers

Source: Dean J. Champion, "Teenage Felons and Waiver Herings: Some Recent Trends, 1980 - 1988." *Crime and Delinquency*, 35 (October 1989), p. 581. Reprinted with permission.

adult courts, this is not likely to occur to many of them, especially property offenders.

Violent offenders present a different case. These are the juveniles for whom the transfer process seems ideally suited. Indeed, many of these youths will be transferred to the adult court (Nimick et al. 1986; Speirs 1989). The question remains, are there appropriate treatment services in existence and available in the adult system for these offenders? The irony associated with these youngsters is that some of them will commit only one offense, albeit a serious one. Therefore, transferring these adolescents to adult court is based on the assumption that there is no hope for their rehabilitation in the juvenile justice system, and that future treatment will need to be provided by the adult system, irrespective of the type and seriousness of the offense. What some states (e.g., Arizona, California, Hawaii,

Table 3.7
Criminal court dispositions of 2,818 waivers, 1980–1988
(percentages rounded)

Year	Dismissed Aquitted	Probation	Jail	Prison	Other[a]
1980	62 (38%)	66 (40%)	11 (7%)	8 (5%)	16 (10%)
1981	65 (36%)	82 (46%)	17 (9%)	7 (4%)	8 (4%)
1982	74 (33%)	107 (47%)	18 (8%)	14 (6%)	13 (6%)
1983	79 (27%)	156 (53%)	28 (9%)	14 (5%)	17 (6%)
1984	92 (24%)	221 (57%)	19 (5%)	17 (4%)	36 (10%)
1985	84 (25%)	195 (58%)	20 (6%)	17 (5%)	21 (6%)
1986	101 (24%)	234 (56%)	25 (6%)	17 (4%)	42 (10%)
1987	87 (21%)	248 (60%)	25 (6%)	21 (5%)	32 (8%)
1988	88 (22%)	249 (62%)	16 (4%)	20 (5%)	29 (7%)
Total	732 (26%)	1,558 (55%)	179 (6%)	135 (5%)	214 (8%)
	Grand Total = 2,818 (100%)				

Source: Dean J. Champion, "Teenage Felons and Waiver Hearings: Some Recent Trends, 1980 - 1988." Crime and Delinquency, 35 (October 1989), p. 583. Reprinted with permission.

[a] Split sentences, home incarceration, electronic monitoring, community-based supervision, etc.

Kansas, and Tennessee) have chosen to do is extend the juvenile court's jurisdiction beyond eighteen years of age. These states view positive treatment outcomes as more likely to occur in the juvenile system rather than in the adult system. The subject of expanded juvenile jurisdiction will be discussed more fully in Chapter 6.

When considering the factors mentioned in concert with the findings of other researchers, it does not appear that juveniles receive harsher penalties, on the average, when transferred to criminal courts for a broad range of offenses. As Rubin (1985:26) suggests, these waivers appear to be cosmetic, primarily public-placating "escape valves" used to rid juvenile courts of chronic recidivists, largely property offenders. Automatic transfer laws in various states such as Florida, Illinois, and New York seem to be having the desired effect, however—although there is an inconsistent pattern that has developed.

Schack and Nessen (1984) reported, for instance, that of 1,817 successful waivers studied by the end of 1983, 33 percent resulted in incarcerative terms no longer than would have been levied in family or juvenile courts had transfers not been initiated. And a study by Reed (1983) of 346 transfers from 1975 to 1981 showed that while most of those transfers involved serious crimes (e.g., murder, rape, and robbery), 66 percent either were dropped, led to acquittals, or were plea-bargained to lesser charges. Singer's (1985) investigation of transfers in New York State also discloses greater use of probation and shorter incarcerative sentences for those juveniles transferred to criminal court. Thus, these so-called "tough, new laws" are not as tough as they appear at first.

SUMMARY

It would seem from the data presented in this chapter and summarized from other sources that waiver of jurisdiction is a policy devoid of substance. The outcome of most transfers appears to be that policies are merely cosmetic rather than effective crime control. The punishment envisioned for transferred juveniles never materializes or it never is quite as severe as expected. As previously mentioned, transfers can be viewed as "eyewash" or "whitewash." Viewing policies as eyewash simply means that they have little substantive impact, but that they are intended to make the world look better. Whitewash gives the impression that things are better than they really are (or that they are different from what they have been). The clear implication is that there is little concern for what these policies can achieve, as long as they look good to the public or make the public think that something is being done about juvenile crime.

Transfers do have sanctioning implications for juvenile offenders, but most of this potential remains unrealized. Gillespie and Norman (1984:34) note, for example, that 53 percent of the juvenile certifications they studied in Utah resulted in short periods of incarceration, or no incarceration at all. The most serious, personal offenders do receive transfers to adult courts, and some receive relatively severe sentences, although these are the exceptions rather than the rule (Champion 1990; Nimick et al. 1986; Speirs 1989). The most frequent recipients of waivers are persistent property offenders, however, and these are the types of delinquents least likely to be incarcerated by adult criminal courts. Thus, the intended policy results desired are not the actual policy results realized as a consequence of juvenile transfers.

NOTE

1. New Mexico, for example, used fifteen as the age of transfer in cases involving homicide, and age sixteen for all other offenses (see New Mexico Statutes Annotated, Sections 32–1–29 and 32–1–30).

CHAPTER 4

Implications of Transfers for Juvenile Offenders

When juveniles are processed by the juvenile justice system, they are exposed to a wide range of punishment options if adjudicated as delinquent. Chapters 2 and 3 outlined the juvenile justice system and the options available to juvenile court judges when administering punishment. This chapter amplifies these discussions and examines certain implications of remaining within the juvenile system compared with a formal transfer to criminal courts.

There are both advantages and disadvantages accruing to youthful offenders, depending upon the course chosen. If they remain in juvenile court or fight the waiver to criminal court, they do not necessarily enjoy the full range of rights and constitutional guarantees associated with adult processing in criminal courts. The proceeding continues to be a civil one, and when these juveniles reach the age of majority, their court records are either suppressed or expunged, thus effectively isolating their previous misdeeds. If the transfer is uncontested, they enter an adult criminal court where their own conduct may be garden-variety, low-risk crime. Judges may even take into account their youthfulness as a mitigating factor, and these youths may be sentenced to probation, have their cases dismissed, or have their sentences suspended.

This chapter examines some of the more important implications for juveniles if they (1) remain in juvenile courts to have their charges resolved, or (2) enter criminal courts to have their alleged offenses adjudicated. The right to a jury trial is optional for some juvenile offenders, depending upon the jurisdiction. By and large, most jurisdictions permit the juvenile judge to exercise discretion about granting trials. In criminal courts, however, jury trials are a matter of right for anyone charged with an offense where the possible punishment involves incarceration of six months or longer. Thus, juveniles may attain advantages in criminal courts that were denied them in certain juvenile court jurisdictions.

Perhaps the most severe sanction criminal courts can impose is the death penalty. The death penalty cannot be imposed by any juvenile court judge in the United States. In order for this maximum punishment to be administered, the youth must be convicted of a capital offense, and the conviction must occur in a state where the death penalty is applicable. This chapter examines the controversy about the death penalty for juveniles and the conditions under which it may be administered. Finally, public policy will be examined as it relates to harsher penalties for juveniles. Are transfers of juveniles to criminal courts desirable? Is the "get tough" policy applicable to juvenile court settings as well as criminal courts (Schwartz 1989)? Some plausible answers to these and other questions will be provided.

IMPLICATIONS OF JUVENILE COURT PROCESSING

Although the jurisdiction of juvenile courts is limited, it should not be underestimated. It is insufficient to categorically conclude that having a case processed by juvenile court is decidedly better than having a criminal court receive and possibly hear the case. By the same token, one cannot say that criminal court processing of an offense is better than juvenile court processing, in any absolute sense. There are advantages and disadvantages associated with both systems, and each must be considered in order to appreciate fully the implications for affected juveniles.

Among the positive benefits of having one's case heard in juvenile court are:

1. juvenile court proceedings are civil, not criminal: thus, juveniles do not acquire criminal records;

2. juveniles are less likely to receive sentences of detention;

3. life imprisonment and the death penalty lie beyond the jurisdiction of juvenile judges, and they cannot impose these harsh sentences;

4. juvenile courts are traditionally more lenient than criminal courts;

5. considerably more public sympathy is extended to those who are processed in the juvenile justice system, despite the general public advocacy for a greater "get tough" policy;

6. compared with criminal courts, juvenile courts do not have as elaborate an information-exchange apparatus to determine whether certain juveniles have been adjudicated delinquent by juvenile courts in other jurisdictions; and

7. compared with criminal court judges, juvenile court judges have considerably more discretion in influencing a youth's life chances prior to or at the time of adjudication.

First, since the juvenile court is exclusively a civil entity, records pertaining to juvenile adjudications are suppressed, expunged, or otherwise deleted whenever juveniles in those jurisdictions reach the age of their majority (Dunn 1986; Michigan Law Review (1983). Second, juvenile judges often act compassionately, either by sentencing youthful offenders to probation, issuing verbal warnings or reprimands, or by imposing some other nonincarcerative, non-fine alternative (Challeen 1986; Conrad 1983).

A third advantage accruing to juveniles is that it is beyond the jurisdiction of juvenile judges to impose life imprisonment and/or the death penalty, despite a potential jury trial scenario (Streib 1987; Thomas and Hutcheson 1986). Thus, if an offender comes before a juvenile judge for processing and has committed an especially aggravated violent or capital offense, the juvenile judge's options are limited. However, if a waiver is initiated successfully, then a path is cleared for possible application of such punishments in criminal courts (Streib 1983). The death penalty applied to juvenile offenders will be examined at length later in this chapter.

A fourth advantage is that juvenile courts are traditionally noted for their lenient treatment of juveniles (Rubin 1988). This seems to be more a function of the influence of priorities in dealing with juvenile offenders, rather than some immovable policy that might impose standard punishments of incarceration as penalties. For example, a national conference of juvenile justice experts in New Orleans, Louisiana recommended that juvenile courts should emphasize three general goals in their adjudication decisions: (1) protection of the community, (2) imposing accountability, and (3) helping juveniles and equipping them to live productively and responsibly in the community (Maloney et al. 1988). This "balanced approach" is largely constructive, in that it heavily emphasizes those skills that lead to the rehabilitation of youthful offenders. And in the minds of many citizens, rehabilitation is equated with leniency. Increasingly used in various jurisdictions, however, are residential placement facilities, where the recidivism rate among juveniles is relatively low compared with those offenders with more extensive histories of delinquent conduct (Goodstein and Southeimer 1987).

A fifth advantage of juvenile court processing is that a significant element among the public advocates sympathy for youths who commit offenses. The prevalent belief is that many juveniles get into trouble because of sociocultural factors which extend well beyond their own abilities and inhibitions. Thus, individualized treatment is necessary, perhaps administered through appropriate community-based facilities, in order to promote greater respect for the law and to offer the needed services where applicable (American Correctional Association 1985; Blackmore et al. 1988; Krisberg 1988; Teschner and Wolter 1984). Some researchers have noted support for a mandatory diversion policy in various jurisdictions, especially where it is applied to less serious youthful offenders and those charged with nonviolent, petty crimes (McDermott et al. 1985). The argument is that many juveniles do not require intensive supervised probation or incarceration, but rather, they simply need a limited amount of responsible supervision to guide them toward and assist them in locating various services and treatment-oriented agencies (McDermott et al. 1985). Not everyone agrees with this view, however (van den Haag 1986).

Finally, juvenile courts do not ordinarily exchange information with most other juvenile courts in a massive national communication network. Local control over youthful offenders accomplishes precisely this limited objective—local control. Therefore, juveniles could conceivably migrate to other jurisdictions and offend repeatedly, although getting caught in those alternative jurisdictions would not be the equivalent of recidivism in one's home jurisdiction. This is of strategic value to juveniles who might seek to commit numerous offenses in a broad range of contiguous jurisdictions. The probability that their acts in one jurisdiction would come to the attention of juvenile officials in their own jurisdiction is remote.

Furthermore, juveniles in certain jurisdictions may reappear before the same juvenile judge frequently. Multiple adjudications for serious offenses do not automatically mean that these youths will be placed in juvenile detention or transferred to criminal court (August 1981). Even those who reappear before the same juvenile judge may be adjudicated repeatedly without significant effect. In one investigation, it was found that a sample of serious juvenile offenders had been adjudicated in the same jurisdiction an average of ten times (Hartstone and Hansen 1984). Thus, there is an inclination on the part of juvenile judges to continue to give juveniles the "benefit of the doubt" and opt for some alternative to detention. Of course, a nondetention alternative is influenced significantly by the degree of crowding in secure juvenile facilities in these jurisdictions. Therefore, the "leniency" of juvenile judges may be more a function of necessity rather than a personal belief that incarceration should be avoided at all costs.

Juvenile courts are not entirely without fault to youthful offenders. Among their several limitations are (1) juvenile courts have the power to administer lengthy incarcerative sentences, not only for serious and dangerous offenders, but for status offenders as well; (2) in most states, juvenile courts are not required to provide juveniles with a jury trial; (3) because of their wide discretion in handling juveniles, judges may underpenalize a large number of those appearing before them on various charges; and (4) juveniles do not enjoy the same range of constitutional rights as adults in criminal courts.

On the negative side, juvenile judges may impose short-term or long-term incarceration in secure juvenile facilities on offenders, regardless of the nonseriousness or pettiness of their offenses. In the case of *In re Gault* (1967), fifteen-year-old Gerald Gault was sentenced to nearly six years in the Arizona State Industrial School for allegedly making an obscene telephone call to a female neighbor (see Chapter 5 for a more in-depth discussion of juvenile rights). An adult committing the same offense would have been fined fifty dollars and may have served thirty days in a local jail. In Gault's case, not only was the sentence excessive, but there were constitutional irregularities. Although this unusual incarcerative sentence was subsequently overturned by the U.S. Supreme Court on numerous constitutional grounds, the fact remains that juvenile judges currently continue to impose similar sentences, provided that the constitutional guarantees assured by the *Gault* decision hold in any particular youth's case.

Another disadvantage of juvenile courts is that granting any juvenile a jury trial may involve a great deal of discretion by prosecutors and juvenile judges. If the judge approves, the juvenile may receive a jury trial in selected jurisdictions, if a jury trial is requested. This practice typifies juvenile courts in thirty-eight states. In the remaining states, juveniles may request and receive trials under certain circumstances. In other words, at least twelve states have made it possible for juveniles to receive jury trials upon request, although the circumstances for such jury trial requests closely parallel the jury trial requests of defendants in criminal courts. Again, we must consider the civil-criminal distinction that adheres respectively to juvenile and criminal court proceedings. Jury trials in juvenile courts retain the civil connotation without causing juveniles to acquire criminal records. However, jury trials in adult criminal courts result in the offender's acquisition of a criminal record, upon conviction.

A third limitation of juvenile proceedings is that the wide discretion enjoyed by most juvenile judges is often abused (Osbun and Rode 1984). This abuse is largely in the form of excessive leniency, and it does not occur exclusively at the adjudicatory stage of juvenile processing. Earlier, during intake, many cases are resolved, diverted, or dismissed without a formal petition being filed for a subsequent adjudication. One investigator has reported that in Maricopa County, Arizona, 17,773 juvenile delinquents who were born between 1962 and 1965 were tracked and determined to have committed over 76,000 delinquent acts (McCarthy 1989). Nearly 90 percent of these juveniles under age sixteen who were referred to juvenile court had their cases disposed of at the intake level. Furthermore, although more serious violent crime cases were more likely to result in incarceration than other offenses, the most frequent disposition was probation. And a majority of those who had committed robbery, aggravated assault, and burglary recidivated within two years of their original adjudications for these offenses (McCarthy 1989).

Because of this leniency and wide discretion, real or imagined, many juvenile courts have drawn criticisms over the years from the public and professionals, alike. The usual allegation is that juvenile courts neglect the accountability issue through the excessive use of probation or diversion (Harris and Graff 1988).

Another major criticism of these courts is that juveniles do not enjoy the full range of constitutional rights applicable to their adult counterparts in criminal courts (Mones 1984; Rubin 1985b; Thomas and Bilchik 1985). In many jurisdictions, there are no transcripts of proceedings against juveniles where serious charges are alleged unless special arrangements are made. Thus, when juveniles in these jurisdictions appeal their adjudications to higher courts, they may not have the written record to rely upon while attempting appellate authority to override the juvenile judge's sentence.

Juvenile Trial Options: Interstate Variations

As we have seen juveniles may or may not receive a trial by jury if their cases are adjudicated by juvenile courts. As of 1988, twelve states legislatively mandated jury trials for juveniles, if requests were made during their adjudicatory hearings. Also in 1988, in 23 other states juveniles were denied the right to a jury trial. In the remaining states, with the exception of South Dakota, no mention was made of whether or not juveniles were entitled to jury trials. It is presumed that in these jurisdictions at least, the sole authority bestowing such a jury trial privilege would be the juvenile judge. In South Dakota, a court order is required for a jury trial to be conducted in juvenile court (Jamieson and Flanagan 1989:156–57). Table 4.1 shows different jury trial provisions in juvenile courts by state.

IMPLICATIONS OF CRIMINAL COURT PROCESSING

When juveniles are transferred to criminal court, then all rules and constitutional guarantees attach for them as well as for adults. We have already examined the advantages of permitting or petitioning the juvenile court to retain jurisdiction in certain cases. The absence

Table 4.1
Interstate variation in jury trials for juveniles, 1988

Provision	States
(1) Jury trial granted upon request by juvenile	Alaska, California, Kansas, Massachusetts, Michigan, Minnesota, New Mexico, Oklahoma, Texas, West Virginia, Wisconsin, Wyoming
(2) Juvenile denied right to trial by jury	Alabama, Florida, Georgia, Hawaii, Indiana, Iowa, Louisiana, Maine, Maryland, Mississippi, Nebraska, Nevada, New Jersey, North Carolina, North Dakota, Ohio, Oregon, Pennsylvania, South Carolina, Tennessee, Utah, Vermont, Washington
(3) No Mention	Alaska, Arizona, California, Colorado, Idaho, Illinois, Missouri, New Hampshire, New Mexico, Virginia
(4) By court order	South Dakota

Source: Katherine M. Jamieson and Timothy J. Flanagan, (eds.). Sourcebook of Criminal Justice Statistics, 1988. Washington DC: U.S. Department of Justice, pp. 156-57.

of a criminal record, limited punishments, extensive leniency, and a greater variety of discretionary options on the part of juvenile judges make juvenile courts an attractive adjudicatory medium, if the juvenile has a choice. Of course, even if the crimes alleged are serious, leniency may assume the form of a dismissal of charges, charge reductions, warnings, and other nonadjudicatory penalties.

The primary implications for juveniles of being processed through the criminal justice system are several, and they are quite important. First, depending upon the seriousness of the offenses alleged, a jury trial may be a matter of right. Second, periods of lengthy incarceration in minimum, medium, and maximum security facilities with adults becomes a real possibility. Third, criminal courts in a majority of state jurisdictions may impose the death penalty in capital cases. This is regarded as the ultimate punishment and is hotly debated as a formal criminal sanction (Doerner 1988; Hochstedler 1986; Scoville 1987; Smith 1986; Smykla 1987).[1] An especially sensitive subject with most citizens is whether juveniles should receive the death penalty if convicted of capital crimes. In recent years, the U.S. Supreme Court has addressed this issue specifically. Subsequently in this chapter, the issue of imposing the death penalty on juveniles will be discussed in depth.[2]

Jury Trials as a Matter of Right for Serious Crimes

A primary benefit of a transfer to criminal court is the right to a jury trial. This is conditional, however, and depends upon the minimum incarcerative period associated with one or more criminal charges filed against defendants. In only twelve state jurisdictions, juveniles have a jury trial right granted through legislative action (Mahoney 1985a). However, when juveniles reach criminal courts, certain constitutional provisions apply to them, as well as to adults. First, anyone charged with a crime where the possible sentence is six months incarceration or more is entitled to a jury trial (*Baldwin v. New York* 1970). Therefore, it is not a discretionary matter resting solely with the judge. Any defendant who *may be* subject to six months or more in prison or jail on the basis of the prescribed statutory punishment associated with the criminal offenses alleged may request and receive a jury trial from any judge, in either state or federal courts.

Juveniles charged with particularly serious crimes, and where several aggravating circumstances are apparent, stand a good chance of favorable treatment from juries. Aggravating circumstances include a victim's death or the infliction of serious bodily injuries, commission of an offense while on bail for another offense or on probation or parole, use of extreme cruelty in the commission of the crime, use of a dangerous weapon in the commission of a crime, a prior record, and leadership in the commission of offenses alleged. However, mitigating circumstances, those factors that tend to lessen the severity of sentencing, include duress or extreme provocation, mental incapacitation, motivation to provide necessities, youthfulness or old age, and no previous criminal record (Just 1985).

No one can predict accurately how juries will decide cases. Although some evidence exists to show the influence of race and gender on jury decision making, it is inconsistent and inconclusive (Clayton 1983; Humphrey and Fogarty 1987; Kempf and Austin 1986; LaFree 1985; Petersilia 1983; Spohn et al. 1985). Impressions gleaned from various surveys of U.S. citizens suggest that age might function favorably to reduce sentencing severity in jury trials. For example, a 1986 survey of 917 Georgia residents disclosed that while three-fourths favored the death penalty, over two-thirds favored replacing the death penalty with life imprisonment as the *maximum punishment* for youthful offenders (Thomas and Hutcheson 1986). Such comparative leniency may be indicative of how juries might view youthful defendants on capital punishment cases as well as those lesser crimes associated with less serious punishments. Thus, youthfulness itself is an inherent mitigating factor in almost every criminal courtroom. It is also important to note that among the several aggravating and mitigating circumstances listed above, having or not having a prior record becomes an important consideration. Youths transferred to criminal courts most likely do not have previous *criminal* records. This does not mean that they have not previously committed crimes, but rather, their records are juvenile court records. As such, technically they do not bring "prior criminal records" into the adult courtroom. This is a favorable factor for juveniles to consider when deciding whether to challenge transfers or have their automatic waivers reversed. An absence of a prior criminal record, together with youthfulness, might be persuasive enough for juries to acquit certain defendants or find them guilty of lesser included offenses. Again, we cannot be certain about the precise influence of one's age on jury decision making (Hans and Vidmar 1986; Hastie et al. 1983).

Another important factor relative to having access to a jury trial is that prosecutors often seek to avoid them, favoring a simpler plea bargain arrangement instead (McDonald 1985). Plea bargaining or plea negotiating is a preconviction bargain between the state and the defendant where the defendant enters a guilty plea in exchange for leniency in the form of reduced charges or less harsh treatment at the time of sentencing (adapted from McDonald 1985:5–6). Plea bargaining in the United States accounts for approximately 90 percent of all criminal convictions (Alschuler 1979; Champion 1987a, 1988, 1989b; Stitt and Siegel 1986).

Jury trials are costly, and the results of jury deliberations are unpredictable. If prosecutors can obtain guilty pleas from transferred juveniles, they assist the state and themselves, in terms of both the costs of prosecution and avoidance of jury whims in youthful offender cases. Also, plea bargaining in transferred juvenile cases often results in convictions on lesser charges, specifically charges that would not have prompted the transfer or waiver from juvenile courts initially (Reed 1983). This is ironic, since it suggests that the criminal justice system is inadvertently sabotaging the primary purpose of juvenile transfers through plea bargaining arrangements that are commonplace for adult criminals.

There is another important consideration worth mentioning. When prosecutorial decisions are made, the sufficiency of evidence to enhance the chances of a successful prosecution should exist and the charges alleged should be serious ones. However, many transferred juveniles are not necessarily the most serious youthful offenders, and the standard of evidence in juvenile courts is not as rigorous as it is in criminal courts. Thus, many transferred cases "crumble" at the outset and are dismissed by the prosecutors themselves (Schack and Nessen 1984). A 1983 study of 6,951 transferred juveniles in New York showed that 68.6 percent had their cases dismissed, were not prosecuted, and had left the court system before the end of the justice process (Schack and Nessen 1984). Furthermore, the same study showed that only 4.2 percent of all juveniles arrested eventually received longer incarcerative sentences than they would have received had they elected to have their cases adjudicated in juvenile courts (Schack and Nessen 1984).

Closely associated with prosecutorial reluctance to prosecute many of these transferred juveniles is the fact that a majority of those transferred are charged with property crimes (August 1981; Champion 1989; Gillespie and Norman 1984). While these cases may stand out from other cases coming before juvenile judges, prosecutors and criminal court judges might regard them as insignificant. Thus, juveniles enter the adult system with "special tags" from juvenile courts, but they become one of many property offenders for criminal processing. Their ages also work in their behalf—improving the chances of having their cases dismissed—or of being acquitted by juries. Most prosecutors wish to reserve jury trials for only the most serious offenders. Therefore, their general inclination is to treat youthful property offenders with greater leniency, or they elect to *nolle pro-sequi* outright.

Incarceration

Arguing that it is cheaper to build more prisons than it is to tolerate a growing crime rate, van den Haag (1986) advocates blanket punishment in criminal courts, for juveniles who have committed crimes. Among other things, van den Haag proposes that parole should be abolished. Contrary sentiment is that there has been an overuse of detention for juveniles (Margolis 1988; Rosner 1988). Also, juveniles who are incarcerated in prisons for adults are more often victimized by other prisoners, compared with those juveniles who are remanded to secure juvenile facilities (Forst 1989). Institutional life is also often difficult for juveniles to accept. A study of 146 juveniles incarcerated in adult facilities by the Texas Department of Corrections disclosed that juvenile inmates were twice as likely to be problem inmates, than adults were—resulting in their failure to work or earn good-time credit (McShane and Williams 1989).

There appears to be strong support for keeping juveniles away from adult prisons and jails, not only because such facilities are less well-equipped to meet juvenile offender needs, but also because a greater range of community-based services exists for juveniles diverted or placed on probation in their respective communities (Griffiths 1988). An offsetting argument is made for preserving incarceration as a punishment, in part because of the intensified fear of apprehension and punishment among juveniles, which may tend to "suppress" their propensity to engage in juvenile rime (Fraser and Norman 1988). This particular view lacks empirical support, however.

The number of incarcerated offenders under age eighteen in state and federal prisons is relatively small—accounting for about .5 percent of all inmates nationally, in 1987 (Innes 1988). In fact, this figure represents a decrease of juvenile inmates from a figure of .9 percent in 1979 (Innes 1988). Thus, the actual amount of incarceration in adult facilities imposed on juveniles processed by criminal courts is unremarkable. At the same time, there has been a gradual increase in the number of juveniles detained for short-term or long-term periods in secure juvenile facilities (Reuterman and Hughes 1984). This is suggestive of a hydraulic effect, where juvenile populations are gradually being reduced within adult institutions, but also where increasing numbers of juveniles are being detained in secure facilities for youths. Thus, the place, rather than the rate, of juvenile incarcerations appears to be changing perceptibly.

Regardless of how few youths are imprisoned in adult facilities, however, the fact of such incarcerations is troubling to more than a few citizens (Carter 1984). Among the arguments opposing juvenile incarceration is that misbehavior and crime in youth are transient, and that with proper guidance, most youths mature and abandon criminality over a relatively short time period (Rutherford 1986).

The possibility of incarceration looms large for those juveniles who, one way or another, reach criminal courts. Many states currently employ presumptive or determinate sentencing guidelines that establish standard punishments for all criminal offenses (Goodstein and Hepburn 1985). While judges in those jurisdictions have some latitude in varying the amount of incarceration, some incarceration must be imposed, especially for those convicted of serious crimes. Of course, age is a mitigating factor for convicted juveniles. Judges may tend to select the low end of the punishment range rather than the high end, when sentencing convicted youths. With some exceptions, the average length of incarceration for juveniles convicted in adult courts is relatively short compared with their adult counterparts convicted of similar offenses (August 1981; Reed 1983; Singer 1985). Furthermore, this average length of incarceration is no longer, or greater than the sentences these affected juveniles would have received, if adjudicated and sentenced to a secure juvenile facility by a juvenile judge (Schack and Nessen 1984). These grounds alone are sufficient to challenge the "get tough" policy of contemporary juvenile courts and the value of certifications to criminal courts.

The Death Penalty: The Ultimate Punishment

The most glaring implication for juveniles transferred to criminal courts is the potential imposition of the death penalty upon their conviction for a capital crime. About two-thirds of the states use capital punishment for prescribed offenses that are especially aggravated. The methods of execution in those states that authorize the death penalty include lethal injection, electrocution, lethal gas, hanging, and firing squad (U.S. Department of Justice 1988a:5). At the beginning of 1988, there were 1,984 prisoners in the United States who were under a sentence of death. Ninety-nine percent of these were males. Less than .5 percent of these were under age twenty (U.S. Department of Justice 1988a:6–7).

The administration of the death penalty as a criminal sanction is not unique to the United States. In fact, a study of 128 nations has disclosed that 87 percent currently authorize the death penalty as a punishment form—an increase from 78 percent in 1979 and 85 percent in 1985 (Weichman and Kendall 1987).

Although the death penalty has long been accepted as a constitutional means to "redress grossly unacceptable antisocial behavior" (Smith 1986), it was temporarily suspended (but not prohibited) in 1972 as the result of the *Furman v. Georgia* decision. This decision by the U.S. Supreme Court criticized the racially discriminatory and arbitrary nature of the death penalty as it was currently being applied in Georgia. For example, many Georgia blacks were being executed for crimes of rape and robbery, whereas white defendants convicted of similar offenses received incarcerative terms, rather than death as punishment. Furthermore, no provisions existed for Georgia juries to consider aggravating and mitigating circumstances associated with the offense. Four years later, Georgia statues were changed to comply with U.S. Supreme Court admonitions and provisions in the case of *Gregg v. Georgia* (1976). A major change in Georgia criminal procedure was the creation of a bifurcated trial, wherein guilt was decided in one phase, and punishment was decided in another. The two-phase nature of jury deliberations permitted jurors to consider any especially aggravating or mitigating circumstances before deciding whether to vote for the death penalty.

An alternative to the death penalty is the life-without-parole option. In 1987, 29 states had life-without-parole provisions for capital offender statutes including aggravated homicide, as well as for habitual or career offender statutes (Cheatwood, 1988). No other penalty in our history has generated the amount of controversy surrounding capital punishment (Acker 1987; Friedlander 1987; Lester 1987; Rogers and Wettstein 1987; Sheleff 1987; Smith 1987; van den Haag and Conrad 1983; Zimring and Hawkins 1986).

Those who favor the death penalty believe strongly that (1) it functions as a deterrent to those contemplating committing capital crimes, (2) it is "just" punishment within the context of the justice philosophy prevalent within criminal justice, (3) it is appropriate punishment in the retributive sense, (4) it is incapacitating from the standpoint of the process of "elimination," and (5) it is economical especially when contrasted with lengthy incarceration.

Those who oppose the death penalty say that (1) it does not function as an effective deterrent to capital crimes; (2) it is barbaric, unbecoming, and uncivilized as a "cruel and unusual punishment;" (3) it is discriminatory on racial, gender, and socioeconomic grounds; and (4) there are more humane alternatives, such as life without parole. In fact U.S. Supreme Court Justices Thurgood Marshall and William J. Brennan regularly enter into the record their categorical opposition to the death penalty administered for whatever reason and under any condition, whenever appeals of death sentences reach the U.S. Supreme Court (Brennan 1986; Burris 1987). Since the pros and cons associated with the imposition of capital punishment are for the most part closely intertwined, they will be examined together.

In his analysis of the relation between capital crimes and the use of the death penalty, Forst (1983) observes that some mild support exists for the death penalty as both a specific and general deterrent to homicides. However, he also suggests that the data are inconclusive, regardless of the argument one adopts, either for or against the use of the death penalty as a deterrent. Noticeably, the bulk of research correlating the death penalty with deterrence or reductions in the homicide rate has revealed the death penalty to be an ineffective deterrent (Bailey 1983, 1984; Decker and Kohfeld 1984, 1987; Rogers and Wettstein 1987).

Whether the death penalty is a "just" punishment or should be imposed retributively and brutally depends upon those surveyed. The families and loved ones of murder victims, with some exceptions, are likely to regard the death penalty favorably compared with the opinions of families and loved ones of the condemned (Radelet 1989; Smith 1986; Smykla 1987; Wallace 1989; Warr and Stafford 1984). Accordingly, Friedlander (1987) has contended that during the past half century, no executions of "innocent persons" have occurred. In fact, Friedlander suggests that the average stay of condemned prisoners on death row awaiting execution, averaging six years, is more of a "cruel and unusual punishment" than executions themselves. Also, attempts have been made to make the death penalty more palatable to the American public; lethal injection is presumably less painful to those executed and therefore potentially more acceptable to society (Draper 1985).

Gregg v. Georgia (1976) was a primary benefit in reducing the arbitrariness with which the death penalty could be applied in Georgia and other states. However, this case did not lessen the accusations from interested professionals and others that racism and other nonlegal factors adversely influence the administration of the death penalty today (Bienen et al. 1988; Ekland-Olson 1988; Gross and Mauro 1984, 1989; Hanson 1988; Iovanni 1987; Vito and Keil 1988).

In a South Carolina study of court records for the 1977–1981 period, for example, the race of both defendants and victims seemed relevant in regard to the seeking of the death penalty by prosecutors (Paternoster 1984). Three hundred homicide cases were examined. Paternoster (1984) found that black killers of whites were far more likely than white killers of blacks, or even black killers of other blacks, to have the death penalty sought. This seems to be a fairly consistent and continuing pattern in the administration of the death penalty. Other confirming evidence has been found for this pattern (Heilbrun et al. 1989). Of course, gender and socioeconomic status have been correlated with the death penalty as well. Disproportionately fewer women than men receive the death penalty, considering all of those eligible to receive it, and some evidence suggests that those convicted offenders are characterized by lower socioeconomic status (Hengstler 1987; Radelet and Vandiver 1983).

Some writers view the use of the death penalty largely from the standpoint of economics. Is capital punishment cost effective relative to long-term incarceration? Although it is clear that each execution makes additional precious prison space available, the value-laden dilemma of executing others, remains (Bedau 1982). Other researchers contend that elimination of capital offenders increases respect for the law. However, elimination is a defensible rationale only if the death penalty is applied frequently, which it is not (Fattah 1985). Fattah argues that incarceration fulfills the elimination function through incapacitation. He finds it difficult to justify to others how official killings by the state can promote respect for human life.

What about convicted murderers who kill others while in prison serving life terms (Vollmann 1987)? Again, there are no easy answers to the dilemma of what to do about "lifers" who kill other prisoners. New York State has provided for a mandatory death penalty in such cases, provided that a bifurcated proceeding occurs before the death sentence is passed. But even such extremes as the mandatory death penalty for convicted murderers who kill others while in prison is regarded in some sectors as arbitrary and discriminatory (Galbo 1985).

The search for alternatives to the death penalty narrows very quickly to life-without-parole arguments and proponents. In 1987, twenty-nine states had life-without-parole provisions (Cheatwood 1988). One fear is that authorities with the power to pardon will commute many of these life sentences to a relatively short term of years, and that many convicted murderers will once again be on the streets, possibly to kill again (Cheatwood 1988). Perhaps the most drastic life-without parole solution has been described by Snellenburg (1986). Snellenburg has suggested that convicted murderers should receive solitary confinement for life, as an alternative to the death penalty. But even those who support life-without-parole solutions consider such an alternative to be "cruel and unusual" (Galbo 1985; Radelet 1989).

Should Minors Be Executed? The Continuing Debate

In 1987 there were 1,772 inmates on death row in U.S. prisons. Of these, 37 were juveniles aged fifteen, sixteen, and seventeen (Streib 1987:xi, xxxiv). Only 2 of these were female, and the majority were black. Georgia has executed the most youths—41, followed by North Carolina and Ohio with 19 juvenile executions each. Only 14 states have never executed youths.

Capital punishment in the United States applied to juveniles under age eighteen is not new. Between 1642 and 1986, there were 281 executions of youths under age eighteen at the time of their conviction offense. While the first execution involved a sixteen-year-old boy, Thomas Granger, who had sodomized a horse and was convicted of bestiality, the youngest person ever executed was ten-year-old James Arcene, convicted of robbing and murdering a victim in Arkansas, in 1855. Because he was not apprehended immediately, he was eventually executed by officials at age twenty-three (Streib 1987:57).

All of the arguments advanced above that function as either pros or cons relative to the death penalty also apply directly to the issue of juvenile executions. However, because of the nature of juvenile justice reforms, a strong belief persists that substantial efforts must be made by juvenile courts and corrections to rehabilitate juveniles, rather than incarcerate or execute them. For example, a study conducted by Amnesty International examined public attitudes toward the death penalty among a sample of 1,400 Florida residents (Cambridge Survey Research 1986). While the survey found overwhelming support for the death penalty, it was also disclosed that most respondents considered the death penalty inappropriate as the ultimate punishment for juvenile offenders convicted of capital crimes. In those states where executions are conducted, where should the line be drawn concerning the minimum age at which someone becomes liable, accountable, and subject to the death penalty?

In recent years, several U.S. Supreme Court cases have been especially significant in providing a legal foundation for executions of juveniles. These include *Eddings v. Oklahoma* (1982), *Thompson v. Oklahoma* (1988), *Stanford v. Kentucky* (1989), and *Wilkins v. Missouri* (1989).

As a prelude to discussing these cases, it should be noted that until 1982, sixteen states had minimum-age provisions for juvenile executions (under age eighteen), where the range in minimum age was from ten (Indiana) to seventeen (Georgia, New Hampshire, and Texas). When the *Eddings v. Oklahoma* case was decided in 1982, the minimum age for juvenile executions in all states was raised to sixteen.

Eddings v. Oklahoma (1982). On April 4, 1977, Monty Lee Eddings and several other companions ran away from their Missouri homes. In a car owned by Eddings's older brother, they drove, without direction or purpose, eventually reaching the Oklahoma Turnpike. Eddings had several firearms in the car, including rifles that he had stolen from his father. At one point, Eddings lost control of the car and was stopped by an Oklahoma State Highway Patrol officer. When the officer approached the car, Eddings stuck a shotgun out of the window and killed the officer outright. When Eddings was apprehended, he was waived to criminal court on a prosecutorial motion. Efforts by Eddings and his attorney to oppose the waiver failed.

In a subsequent trial, several aggravating circumstances were introduced and alleged, while several mitigating circumstances, including Eddings's youthfulness, mental state, and potential for treatment were considered by the trial judge. However, the judge did not consider Eddings's "unhappy upbringing and emotional disturbance" as significant mitigating factors to offset the aggravating ones. Eddings's attorney filed an appeal which eventually reached the U.S. Supreme Court. Although the Oklahoma Court of Criminal Appeals reversed the trial judge's ruling, the U.S. Supreme Court reversed the Oklahoma Court of Criminal Appeals. The reversal pivoted on whether the trial judge erred by refusing to consider the "unhappy upbringing and emotionally disturbed state" of Eddings. The trial judge previously had acknowledged the youthfulness of Eddings as a mitigating factor. The *fact* of Eddings's age, sixteen, was significant, precisely because the majority of justices did not consider it significant. Rather, they focused upon the issue of introduction of mitigating circumstances specifically outlined in Eddings's appeal. Oklahoma was now in the position of lawfully imposing the death penalty on a juvenile who was sixteen years old at the time he committed murder.

Thompson v. Oklahoma (1988). William Wayne Thompson was convicted of murdering his former brother-in-law, Charles Keene. Keene had been suspected of abusing Thompson's sister. On the evening of January 22–23, 1983, Thompson and three older companions left his mother's house, saying "We're going to kill Charles." Facts disclose that in the early morning, Charles Keene was beaten to death by Thompson and his associates with fists and hand-held weapons, including a length of pipe. Thompson later told others, "We killed him. I shot him in the head and cut his throat in the river." Thompson's accomplices told police shortly after their arrest that Thompson had shot Keene twice in the head, and then cut his body in several places (e.g., throat, chest, and abdomen), so that, according to Thompson, "the fish could eat his body." When Keene's body was recovered on February 18, 1983, the medical examiner indicated that Keene had been shot twice in the head, had been beaten, and that his throat, chest, and abdomen had been cut.

Since Thompson was fifteen years old at the time of the murder, juvenile officials transferred his case to criminal court. This transfer was supported, in part, by an Oklahoma statutory provision indicating that there was "prosecutive merit" in pursuing the case against Thompson. Again, the subject of the defendant's youthfulness was introduced as a mitigating factor (among other factors), together with aggravating factors such as the "especially heinous, atrocious, and cruel" manner in which Keene had been murdered. Thompson was convicted of first-degree murder and sentenced to death.

Thompson filed an appeal which eventually reached the U.S. Supreme Court. The Court examined Thompson's case at length, and in a vigorously debated opinion, overturned Thompson's death sentence, indicating in its conclusory dicta that

"petitioner's counsel and various *amici curiae* have asked us to "draw the line" that would prohibit the execution of any person who was under the age of eighteen at the time of the offense. Our task, today, however, is to decide the case before us; we do so by concluding that the Eighth and Fourteenth Amendments prohibit the execution of a person who was under sixteen years of age at the time of his or her offense (108 S.Ct. at 2700).

Accordingly, Thompson's death penalty was reversed. Officially, this Supreme Court action effectively drew a temporary line of sixteen years of age as a minimum for exacting the death penalty in capital cases. This "line" awaited subsequent challenges, however.

Stanford v. Kentucky (1989). Kevin Stanford was seventeen when, on January 17, 1981, he and an accomplice repeatedly raped, and sodomized, and eventually shot to death twenty-year-old Baerbel Poore in Jefferson County, Kentucky. This occurred during a robbery of a gas station where Poore worked as an attendant. Stanford later told police, "I had to shoot her [since] she lived next door to me and she would recognize me... I guess we could have tied her up or something or beat [her up]... and tell her if she tells, we would kill her...."·A corrections officer who interviewed Stanford said that after Stanford made that disclosure, "he [Stanford] started laughing." The jury in Stanford's case found him guilty of first-degree murder, and the judge sentenced him to death. The U.S. Supreme Court eventually heard his appeal, and in an opinion which addressed the "minimum age for the death penalty" issue, decided both this case and the case of Heath Wilkins.

Wilkins v. Missouri (1989). Heath Wilkins, a sixteen-year-old at the time of the crime, stabbed to death Nancy Allen Moore, a twenty-six-year-old mother of two who was working behind the counter of a convenience store in Avondale, Missouri. On July 27, 1985, Wilkins and his accomplice, Patrick Stevens, entered the convenience store to rob it, agreeing with Wilkins's plan that they would kill "whoever was behind the counter" because "a dead person can't talk." When the entered the store, they stabbed Moore, who fell to the floor. When Stevens had difficulty opening the cash register, Moore, mortally wounded, offered to help him. Wilkins stabbed her three more times in the chest, two of the knife wounds penetrating Moore's heart. Moore began to beg for her life, whereupon Wilkins stabbed her four more times in the neck, opening up her carotid artery. She died shortly thereafter. Stevens and Wilkins netted $450 in cash and checks, some liquor, cigarettes, and rolling papers, from the robbery/ murder. Wilkins was convicted of first-degree murder, and the judge sentenced him to death.

As has been indicated above, the U.S. Supreme Court heard both cases at once, since the singular issue was whether the death penalty was considered cruel and inhumane as it pertained to sixteen- and seventeen-year-olds. At that time, not all states had reached consensus concerning the application of the death penalty for persons under the age of eighteen. Although several justices dissented from the majority view, the U.S. Supreme Court upheld the death sentences of Stanford and Wilkins, concluding that "we discern neither a historical nor a modern societal consensus forbidding the imposition of capital punishment on any person who murders at sixteen or seventeen years of age. Accordingly, we conclude that such punishment does not offend the Eight Amendment's prohibition against cruel and unusual punishment" (109 S.Ct. at 2980). Thus, this crucial opinion underscored sixteen as the minimum age at which the death penalty may be administered.

There has been extensive dialogue concerning the juvenile death penalty issue (Just 1985; Markman and Cassell 1988; Polen 1987; Ricotta 1988; Streib 1987, 1988; Wallace 1989). Beyond the question of whether the death penalty should be administered at all to anyone, there is no apparent consensus concerning the application of the death penalty to juveniles convicted of capital crimes. Arguments favoring the death penalty stress the accountability of these youthful offenders and the justice of capital punishment where capital crimes have been committed. Arguments opposing the death penalty for juveniles are often emotionally laden or address issues related only remotely to the death penalty issue (Brodie 1986; Ellison 1987; Polen 1987; Wilson 1983). For instance, it is argued that juveniles are more amenable to treatment and rehabilitation, and thus, provisions should be made for this rehabilitation and treatment to occur (Wilson 1983). Whatever the appeal of such an argument, the U.S. Supreme Court has, at least for the time being, resolved the age/death penalty issue with some degree of finality. Other factors will have to be cited as mitigating in a youth's defense, if a capital crime is alleged.

PUBLIC POLICY IMPLICATIONS

Because of the relatively small number of juveniles on death rows in U.S. state prisons, and because of the declining frequency with which juveniles have been executed in recent years, the death penalty issue applied to juveniles does not seem to be as strong as it once was. There will always be a significant segment of society that will continue to oppose the death penalty for whatever reason. But until substantial shifts occur in the composition of the present U.S. Supreme Court, it is doubtful that major changes will be made relative to death penalty policy applied to juvenile capital offenders.

While public sentiment is not always easy to measure or gauge, there does appear to be strong sentiment for harsher penalties meted out to juveniles. This does not necessarily mean the death penalty or life imprisonment, but it does mean tighter laws and enforcement of those laws where juveniles are concerned. Several issues related to public sentiment regarding juvenile punishment follow. Also assessed are political sentiments toward the juvenile punishment issue.

Public Sentiment and Harsher Penalties for Juveniles

The views of professionals in criminal justice and criminology are not that dissimilar from the views held by the general public about juvenile delinquency and what should be done to prevent or punish it. Victor Streib (1987:189) has summarized succinctly a commonly expressed, though nebulous, solution that "our society must be willing to devote enormous resources to a search for the causes and cures of violent juvenile crime, just as we have done in the search for the causes and cures of such killer diseases as cancer. And we must not demand a complete cure in a short time, since no one knows how long it will take." Obviously, we have not cured cancer. We are even further away from discovering the etiology of delinquent behavior, in all of its diverse forms, and finding one or more satisfactory cures for it.

One bit of intervention proposed by professionals is the early identification of chronic or hardcore delinquents in a multiple gating technique (Loeber and Dishion 1987). This technique purportedly identifies extreme cases in terms of frequency, variety, seriousness, age of onset, and the number of settings in which the behavior tends to occur. Thus, antisocial and "delinquency-prone" youths may be identified early in their delinquent careers, and appropriate intervention programs may be applied to certain youths selectively. This selectivity is more cost effective in the long run, compared with more costly programs that are generally applicable to youths, regardless of their offense behaviors or personal characteristics (Loeber and Dishion 1987). However, a social experiment covering a two-year period and involving a small number of hardcore juvenile offenders was not particularly optimistic about intensive, specialized treatment and intervention as delinquency prevention forms (Gelber 1988). Even where high quality staff are made available to youths 24 hours a day, 7 days a week without limitation on time or cost, and where the family's needs (e.g., jobs, food, health care, housing, schooling) were met, a majority of these "assisted" youths reverted to criminal conduct, were convicted, and sent to prison (Gelber 1988). Does any form of intervention really work for offenders? We simply do not know at this point.

Those who favor a separate and distinct juvenile justice system contend that the primary goal of juvenile courts should be individualized treatment, with therapy and rehabilitation as dominant factors (Dwyer and McNally 1987). However, other voices encourage perpetuating a separate juvenile justice system which not only is designed to treat and prevent delinquency, but is also designed to hold juveniles strictly accountable for their actions (Springer 1987). Thus, it is suggested that less use be made of incarceration, and greater use be made of probation and parole, with the primary objectives of offering restitution to victims, compensating communities and courts for the time taken to process cases, and performing community services to learn valuable lessons (Maloney et al. 1988; Rubin 1988).

There is no question that the "get tough" movement is still in force and is pervasive throughout the juvenile justice system. One indication of this is the increased use of waivers, as more juveniles are shifted to the jurisdiction of criminal courts. We have seen certain implications of juveniles as they enter criminal courts for processing, although some of these implications are not entirely unfavorable. (A discussion of the influx of large numbers of transferred juveniles into criminal courts will be presented in Chapter 5.)

Increasing numbers of juvenile court judges are soliciting the involvement of community members to assist, in voluntary capacities, in monitoring adjudicated youths. Greater responsibilities are shifting toward parents in many jurisdictions, particularly when their children commit crimes against property and do extensive damage, monetarily (National Council of Juvenile and Family Court Judges 1986).

Public policy currently favors protecting juveniles as much as possible from the stigmatization of courts and criminal labeling, including the large-scale removal of youths from jails and prisons (Georgia Commission on Juvenile Justice 1985; Greenwood 1986; Mones 1984). Accordingly, recommendations from the public include greater use of nonsecure facilities and programs as opposed to detention in secure facilities (Conti et al. 1984). Especially manifest is the concern for very young offenders. More children under age ten are entering the juvenile justice system annually (Sametz 1984). Clearly, effective programs and procedures for processing such youths need to be in place and operative. Encouragement for greater use of community-based services and treatment programs, special education services, and school-based, early intervention programs is apparent (Sametz 1984; Steinhart 1988).

As we have also seen, there is increasing bureaucratization of juvenile courts, indicated in part by greater formality of juvenile case processing. Juvenile proceedings are increasingly adversarial proceedings, similar to criminal courts. Almost all of the criminal court trappings are found in juvenile courts, with some significant exceptions that have been noted previously (Feld 1987b; Sutton 1985).

Most juvenile courts are not courts of record, and much informality exists regarding calling witnesses and offering testimony. Federal and state rules of evidence are relaxed considerably and do not attach directly to juvenile civil proceedings. However, in some jurisdictions where prosecutorial presence has been increased greatly (as one indication of greater bureaucratization of juvenile courts), little perceptible impact upon juvenile processing was observed (Laub and MacMurray 1987).

Juvenile courts are sometimes classified according to a "traditional" or "family model" and "due process" distinction (Ito 1984; Watkins 1987). The traditional courts tend to perpetuate the doctrine of parens patriae, and juvenile judges retain a good deal of discretion in adjudicating offenders. They rely more heavily on detention as a punishment. The "due process" juvenile courtroom relies more heavily on preadjudicatory interactions between defense counsels and prosecutors, and non judicial handling of cases is more the rule, rather than the exception. More frequently used in such courts are nonsecure facilities, community-based programs, probation, and diversion with conditions (Ito 1984).

Politicians' Views of Public Sentiment and Juvenile Policy

The political approach to punishing juveniles is to rely heavily on the sentiments expressed by voting constituencies. State legislators are at the helm of juvenile justice reforms currently, and several organizations are in strategic positions to offer their guidance and assistance in formulating new juvenile policies. The American Bar Association, the American Legislative Exchange Council, and the Institute of Judicial Administration have provided legislators with model penal codes and proposed juvenile court revisions to introduce consistency throughout an inconsistent juvenile justice system (American Bar Association 1986; Orlando et al. 1987; Treanor and Volenik 1987).

The federally funded Juvenile Justice Reform Project, which has reviewed existing juvenile codes and statutes in all fifty states, has conducted an extensive national opinion survey of child-serving professionals (Rossum et al. 1987). Two model juvenile justice acts have been proposed—the Model Delinquency Act and the Model

Disobedient Children's Act. Among other things, these acts, respectively, distinguish between delinquents and status offenders and make provisions for their alternative care, treatment, and punishment. Both acts are designed to hold juveniles responsible for their behavior and to hold the system accountable for its treatment of these youths, as well (Rossum et al. 1987).

Not everyone agrees that these codes are functional and in the best interests of those youths served, however. Some critics say that these codes will weaken the current protection extended to dependent children or children in need of supervision. Furthermore, a serious erosion of judicial discretion may occur, accompanied by increased use of pretrial detention for juveniles where serious crimes are alleged. Also, status offenders may be jailed for violating court orders (Orlando et al. 1987). Indeed, it is difficult to devise a code of accountability founded on the principle of "just deserts" and which performs certain traditional treatment functions in the context of parens patriae (Treanor and Volenik 1987). Additionally, codes of any kind promote a degree of "blind conformity," or compliance with rules for the sake of compliance. With greater codification of juvenile procedures, less latitude exists for judges and others to make concessions and impose individualized sentences where appropriate. The very idea of "individualized" sentences, while appealing to "just deserts" interests, invites abuse through discriminatory treatment on racial, ethnic, gender, and socioeconomic grounds.

Judges themselves see the juvenile court as attempting to instill within youths a respect for the law and help them to assume greater responsibility for their actions (Challeen 1986). Interestingly, this represents a dramatic shift from the policy where juveniles were considered victims of the system and thus less accountable for their actions. The emphasis, currently, is on a policy that identifies delinquents as offenders deserving of punishment (McDermott and Laub 1987). However, current juvenile court organizational structure and the prevalent rehabilitative orientation among those who work with and process juveniles present various obstacles to prosecutorial effectiveness and ensuring that "just deserts" will be realized for youths charged with serious offenses (Laub and MacMurray 1987). One final observation is in order before concluding this chapter. Despite the intent of juvenile sentencing reforms to create harsher sanctions as general deterrents to juvenile delinquency, the juvenile justice system continues to be viewed as a lenient system by prosecutors, legislators, and the public (Harris 1988; Steinhart 1988).

SUMMARY

For juveniles aged sixteen and seventeen who are charged with serious crimes there is a good chance they will be waived to criminal court jurisdictions by juvenile courts. In some states such as New York and Illinois, automatic transfers occur for specific kinds of serious offenses. Juveniles may challenge these transfers or waivers, although there are both advantages and disadvantages associated with such challenges.

Remaining in juvenile court means that any and all records relating to delinquency adjudication will be sealed when juveniles reach the age of majority. This age is eighteen in some states and twenty-one in others. Juvenile courts are civil proceedings; thus, it is not possible for juveniles to acquire criminal records if they are processed in these courts. However, being treated as juveniles means that they do not enjoy the full range of constitutional rights and guarantees available in adult criminal courts. But juvenile courts are traditionally noted for their leniency. Even in instances of excessive recidivism, certain delinquent offenders are continually placed on probation rather than confined. Juvenile correctional facilities are frequently overcrowded, as are their adult prison and jail counterparts. Also, having one's case heard in juvenile court expands greatly the variety of treatment options and community-based services available to youths.

In criminal courts, however, juveniles are extended the full range of rights available to adults. But in such courts, convictions (adjudications of guilt, in this instance) mean criminal records. One advantage for juveniles is that they may request and receive a trial by jury, provided their possible punishment involves incarceration of six months or longer. In most juvenile courts, they enjoy no such jury trial option, except with judicial approval. Jury trials are regarded by some experts as advantageous to youths, since jury members take into account one's youthfulness as a mitigating circumstance. Furthermore, when juveniles appear before judges in criminal courts, their "crimes" do not seem to be as serious as they were regarded to be by juvenile judges. Rather, many older offenders are charged

with the same crimes. Crowded court dockets and overworked prosecutors often mean dismissals of cases, plea bargaining resulting in
probation, and little, if any, hard time behind bars. The juvenile's
youthfulness also functions as a mitigating factor. Many juveniles are
aware of this and take advantage of the system by not fighting waivers
in juvenile court. More often than not, their patience is rewarded
through diversion, probation, or case dismissal.

A major danger accruing to juveniles accused of capital crimes,
however, is that the death penalty may be imposed. While it is only
infrequently imposed on juveniles generally, it nevertheless becomes
an option, particularly if the youth was sixteen years of age or older
when the instant capital offense was alleged. The death penalty has
prompted much controversy. Its proponents believe it to be "just"
punishment, retributive, a crime deterrent, and a method of rime
control through elimination. Its opponents regard it as barbaric,
serving no useful purpose, and violating one's constitutional right to
avoid "cruel and unusual punishment." The issue remains unresolved.

Whether minors should be executed, and the age at which they
can be executed has been addressed by the U.S. Supreme Court. In
several sweeping decisions during the 1980s, the Supreme Court
eventually settled on a minimum age of sixteen, where the death
penalty could be applied. Thus, any juvenile who was sixteen or
older at the time of the offense becomes eligible for the death penalty
in those states which have the death penalty as a punishment. The
public is divided about this issue, as are politicians. Currently, the
juvenile justice system is targeted for numerous reforms, including
a new sentencing system, greater uniformity in the laws of diverse
jurisdictions, and a more consistent concept of what constitutes delinquent conduct. Both public and political sentiment seem to favor
the continuation of juvenile courts, but with measured accountability
through greater use of restitution, community service, and limited
use of detention.

NOTES

1. For an excellent, readable summary of major arguments for or against
the death penalty, see van den Haag and Conrad (1983).

2. An extensive treatment of this subject is found in Streib (1987).

CHAPTER 5

Criminal Court and Juvenile Offender Dispositions

This chapter explores the nature of criminal courts, their goals and functions, as well as the types of offenders who are processed through them.[1] Criminal courts have broad powers for adjudicating cases, either through bench trials or jury trials. As we have seen, nearly 90 percent of all guilty pleas entered in criminal courts have been elicited through plea bargaining. Despite the proportionately smaller number of cases that actually reach criminal courts, there are still judicial docket overloads that glut the system. A small, yet growing, proportion of cases diverted to criminal courts involve transferred juveniles. For many criminal court judges, this growing influx of juveniles into their courtrooms exacerbates speedy trial problems and limits the efficiency and effectiveness with which cases are dispatched.

In earlier chapters we have seen the gradual merger of selected juvenile and adult constitutional rights through several landmark U.S. Supreme Court decisions as well as the growing bureaucratization and formalization of juvenile proceedings. Obviously, there are trade-offs for juveniles who are transferred to adult courts, compared with having their cases adjudicated in juvenile courts. Thus, some of the more important legal rights of juveniles will be examined, particularly as these rights currently differ from those enjoyed by adults in criminal courts.

CRIMINAL COURTS

In all jurisdictions, both state and federal, criminal courts exist to hear and decide cases. The federal district court is the major trial court with jurisdiction over all federal crimes. It also doubles as a civil court, where civil cases make up the bulk of those heard by federal judges and juries. In fact, criminal cases make up less than 15 percent of all cases heard in federal courts annually (Champion 1987a). For lesser federal crimes, the U.S. Magistrate ordinarily presides and decides cases that would otherwise be heard by federal judges.

State judicial systems vary dramatically among jurisdictions. No single plan is followed by all states specifying how their criminal and civil courts are or should be organized or labeled (Dahlin 1986). However, an inspection of a broad array of state courts that hear criminal cases discloses several popular designations, including criminal courts, district courts, superior courts, circuit courts, and supreme courts. These state trial courts may have criminal jurisdiction exclusively, or they may have general jurisdiction that encompasses civil proceedings.

There are different *levels* of courts as well, major and minor trial courts, where courts at lower levels in the judicial hierarchy adjudicate less serious cases. The higher trial courts, or major courts are also *courts of record*, where a written or audio recording is made of court proceedings. These records may be reproduced later if offenders are convicted and decide to appeal their cases on various grounds. Often, higher courts function as appellate bodies for cases appealed from lower court decisions or verdicts. In some states, particularly in geographical areas that are not heavily populated, circuit judges preside at designated times each month in remote regions, to hear and decide a wide range of both civil and criminal matters.

Regardless of what the particular court that hears and decides criminal cases is called, certain constitutional rights attach for all criminal defendants. Several of these important rights are usually outlined for suspects in a "Miranda warning" by law enforcement officers (*Miranda v. Arizona* 1966). Thus, all criminal suspects should be advised that at the time of their arrest:

1. they have the right to an attorney;
2. if they cannot afford an attorney, one will be appointed for them by the court;
3. they may remain silent or elect to answer police questions;
4. if they choose to answer questions, they are permitted to have their attorney present during all phases of questioning;
5. if they give up their right to remain silent, statements they make to police and others may be recorded and used against them later in court; and
6. they may elect to discontinue questioning by police at any time.

If any of these rights are violated when suspects are arrested and charged with a crime, such violations may result in a dismissal of charges against these defendants on purely technical grounds, and certain types of evidence seized by police concurrent with the arrest may be suppressed by judges. These "purely technical grounds" refer to important constitutional rights violations, despite the probable guilt or substance of evidence against the defendant. Some experts have advocated that in order to avoid such technical violations, all arrested suspects should have a "nonwaivable right" to consult with an attorney before being interrogated by police (Ogletree 1987).

Whenever defendants are convicted of a crime, whether through a judge's decision or a jury verdict, a sequence of appeals to higher courts may be invoked by defendants and their attorneys, in both state and federal systems. If constitutional issues are involved in some of these appeals, the likelihood is great that the case will eventually reach the U.S. Supreme Court, sometimes known as the "court of last resort."

However, because of the large number of cases that reach the Supreme Court annually and the limited time in which to decide such cases, the Court eventually hears and writes opinions in about only 5 percent of these cases and rejects the remaining 95 percent of them. It requires a vote of four or more Supreme Court justices to agree to hear any case initially. Thus, no specific justice can impose his or her will on the rest of the Court outright. It is largely through appeals to the U.S. Supreme Court that various constitutional rights for both adults and juveniles have been interpreted and clarified over the years. Particularly important are so-called landmark cases that establish a historical precedent. Therefore, state and federal courts are generally obligated to follow precedents established by the U.S. Supreme Court pertaining to adult and juvenile constitutional rights, when strikingly similar cases are being heard. This precedent-setting doctrine is known legally as *stare decisis*, and all lower federal, state, and local courts must follow U.S. Supreme Court precedents whenever factually similar cases are being decided.

Goals and Functions of Criminal Courts

All criminal courts employ adversarial proceedings. Although this adversarial system has at times been attacked by critics as being "too adversarial" and allegedly slows the process of adjudicating cases, most professionals concur that the adversarial system should be preserved rather than changed (Schulhofer 1986). Thus, if defendants are indigent or are otherwise unable to afford a defense attorney, the trial court will appoint a public defender for them (McIntyre 1987). Those able to pay for their own defense are entitled to counsel at all critical stages of their criminal processing as well (Kittel 1987).

The goals and functions of all criminal courts are fairly uniform. The major aims of criminal courts (encompassing also those courts with general jurisdiction and which hear both civil and criminal cases) include (1) providing an open and impartial forum within which to hear cases, (2) protecting the rights of all criminal defendants and (3) promoting fundamental fairness and justice by issuing sentences commensurate with the nature and seriousness of conviction offenses.

The major functions of criminal courts are largely procedural in nature. Since most guilty pleas in the United States are obtained through plea-bargain agreements, the court must function to approve or reject these agreements in hearings. Judges must oversee these plea-bargain agreements and insure the voluntariness of guilty pleas as well as ascertain the factual basis for them. Since guilty pleas entered through plea-bargain agreements involve waivers of many important constitutional rights (e.g., the right to confront and cross-examine witnesses, the right against self-incrimination, the right to a jury trial, and the right to be found guilty beyond a reasonable doubt), these proceedings have serious implications for defendants. Thus, judges must make every effort to ensure that due process has been or is being observed. Additionally, judges must make rulings pertaining to the admissibility or inadmissibility of evidence. In short, they must effectively preserve the integrity of the court by ensuring that all procedural safeguards are observed in the prosecution and defense of any defendant.

Prior to a formal court proceeding, district attorneys are presented with numerous cases involving a wide variety of criminal charges against an equally wide variety of defendants. These prosecutors must decide which cases to pursue. Case "screening" substantially reduces the number of cases that are subsequently handled by any particular court. Those cases not pursued often are characterized by insufficiency of evidence, unreliability of witnesses, and a host of other factors. Some critics have alleged that prosecutors indulge, either deliberately or inadvertently, in case screening according to race, ethnicity, socioeconomic status, and other extralegal factors, where minority or lower-income defendants are subject to prosecution more frequently than upper-class whites (Spohn et al. 1987). There is no question that prosecutors enjoy considerable latitude in deciding whether to prosecute cases. Furthermore, their decisions are not generally subject to judicial approval and widespread public scrutiny. In fact, the general public almost never knows when cases against certain defendants are dropped, or the reasons for these *nolle prosequis*.

In many jurisdictions, prosecutors may invoke the privilege of diverting certain defendants, temporarily, from the criminal justice system. Diversion ordinarily requires approval from the court, and is often used for first-offenders who have committed minor offenses. Diversion also may include conditions, such as attending driver's education classes for driving while intoxicated or under the influence of alcohol or drugs cases, observance of curfews, securing or continuing employment, payment of maintenance fees and/or victim compensation, community service, restitution, and involvement in specific treatment programs (e.g., drug or alcohol withdrawal, group therapy). Divertees in some jurisdictions may have their records expunged at the conclusion of their diversionary period, whereas in other jurisdictions, the seriousness of the charges is mitigated by the successful completion of diversion.

Those cases that eventually reach the courtroom are tried with or without a jury. As already noted, jury trials are a matter of right to any defendant charged with an offense that is accompanied by possible incarceration for six months or longer upon conviction. If a jury trial is a matter of right for particular defendants, they may waive this right and elect to have the judge decide the case in a bench trial. Rules of criminal procedure in all jurisdictions govern court conduct at each stage of a trial proceeding. Rules of evidence also are applicable. These rules regulate the nature and types of evidence that may be presented. These rules also designate the types of witnesses who may testify and the specific boundaries of their testimony. Judges attempt to ensure that all of these rules are precisely observed at all stages of the trial proceedings. However, not all judges are equally adept in the law, and several types of errors (e.g., plain, harmless, reversible) may be committed. Any types of errors may be cited later on appeal by defense counsels whenever their defendants are convicted. Appellate courts may or may not act and rule favorably (i.e., in the defendant's favor) on these appeals.

When defendants are convicted, either by a bench trial or a jury trial, it is the responsibility of the judge to affix punishment and impose an appropriate sentence. Judges exercise wide latitude in the sentences they impose, and they may impose maximum fines and incarcerative sentences, probation, or some optional intermediate punishment (McCarthy 1987b). When probation or an intermediate punishment is imposed, judges ordinarily retain jurisdiction over convicted offenders for the duration of these conditional sentences. However, when offenders are sentenced to jail or prison for a term of months or years, the jurisdiction over offenders shifts or is passed to correctional authorities, including jail and prison administrations and parole boards. These authorities may decide to grant inmates early release at some later point in time. These early releases are most often conditional, and jurisdiction over these offenders remains with the particular paroling authority.

Therefore, criminal courts are able to exercise many options at various stages of criminal proceedings. When juveniles are transferred or waived to the jurisdiction of criminal courts, they become susceptible to all of these options. Furthermore, their cases fall within the purview of all applicable rules of criminal procedure and evidence, and they are protected by all constitutional guarantees and rights extended to adult offenders.

TYPES OF OFFENDERS IN CRIMINAL COURTS

The types of offenders appearing before judges in criminal courts range from petty offenders (e.g., larceny, petty theft, burglary, vehicular theft) to those charged with armed robbery, rape, aggravated assault, and capital crimes involving the possible imposition of the death penalty. Including waived juveniles, the age range of these offenders is broad, although 25 percent are under twenty-five years of age, while about 75 percent are under thirty-five years of age (Innes 1988).

Acknowledging that (1) most felony arrests do not result in trial (four out of every 100 arrests result in trials), (2) that most guilty pleas are obtained through plea bargaining where various forms of leniency are extended, and (3) that most trials by jury result in conviction (Bureau of Justice Statistics 1988), we are in a good position to better understand the conviction-offense profile of state prison inmates. Less than one-half of 1 percent of these state prison inmates are under age eighteen (Innes 1988). And since this "under age eighteen" figure has either remained unchanged or diminished proportionately in most jurisdictions between 1979 and 1987, we may conclude that large-scale waivers of juveniles to criminal courts during the 1980s have affected state prison populations imperceptibly.

Depending on the jurisdiction, the proportion of convicted felons who are sent to prison or jail for one or more years ranges anywhere from 30 percent to 75 or 80 percent (Bureau of Justice Statistics 1988). Among several other states, California places large numbers of convicted felons on probation rather than incarcerating them, for example (Petersilia 1985). These high probation figures are largely due to prison/jail overcrowding in these jurisdictions. Over 95 percent of all incarcerated state prison inmates are male, about half are black, and a majority are single and have not completed high school. By the end of 1986, violent offenders represented 55 percent of all state prison populations, while property offenders accounted for 31 percent, and drug offenders accounted for 9 percent (Innes 1988). The most common violent crimes characterizing state prisoners were robbery (21 percent) and murder (11 percent) (Innes 1988).

Regarding those placed on probation or in intermediate punishment programs—approximately 38 percent of all probationers, in 1985, were property offenders (Cunniff 1987). Thus, contrary to a prevalent belief among the public, probation is not exclusively extended to low-risk, nonviolent felons. For instance, in 1985, 25 percent of all those convicted of aggravated assault were placed on probation, about 15 percent of those convicted of robbery and rape were granted probation, and 8 percent of those convicted of homicide were placed in probation programs (Cunniff 1987). Therefore, focusing primarily upon felons and the characteristics of those who either plea-bargain or elect the trial option, the profile of convicted offenders, either incarcerated or placed in probation programs, is not remarkably different from the general profile of those who have their cases adjudicated in criminal courts (Champion 1987c, 1988).

THE INTRUSION OF JUVENILES INTO CRIMINAL COURTS

In view of the types of cases that eventually reach criminal courts for disposition and the way those cases are ultimately concluded, it would seem that juvenile court prosecutors and judges would be highly selective in the cases they designate for waiver. Ideally, those cases selected for waiver or transfer would be only the most serious cases, where the charges pending against juveniles would primarily consist of violent crimes such as homicide, rape, robbery, and aggravated assault. Indeed, in some jurisdictions, it works this way. For instance, a 1984 New Jersey survey of juvenile cases prosecutorially waived to adult courts showed that prosecutors' motions for waiver generally involved violent crimes (New Jersey Division of Criminal Justice 1985). Of those cases waived, the majority resulted in guilty pleas through plea bargaining. Of those cases that went to trial, over 70 percent resulted in guilty verdicts, with 95 percent of these involving incarcerative terms (New Jersey Division of Criminal Justice 1985).

And in states such as New York and Illinois, where automatic transfers of certain serious juvenile offenders are statutory, comparatively larger numbers of serious offenders are waived to criminal courts, contrasted with those states without automatic transfer provisions (August 1981; Sagatun et al. 1985). Reed (1983) has shown, for example, that of the offenses charged against transferred juveniles in Illinois between 1978 and 1981, 49 percent were for murder, 22 percent for robbery, and 14 percent for rape.

However, abundant evidence exists to show that in many jurisdictions, particularly those without automatic transfer provisions, transferred juveniles primarily consist of property offenders or those charged with nonviolent, petty crimes (Bishop et al. 1989; Bortner 1986; Nimick et al. 1986). In a 1982 study of 2,335 prosecutorial and judicial waivers in 552 courts in Arizona, California, Hawaii, Iowa, Kansas, Mississippi, Pennsylvania, Tennessee, and Virginia, only one-third of those youths transferred to criminal courts were charged with an index violent offense (Nimick et al. 1986). Most waived cases involved index property offenses, particularly burglary. Also in these jurisdictions transfers accounted for only two percent of all petitioned cases.

Gillespie and Norman (1984) and Bortner (1986) have reached similar conclusions. In their investigation of Utah certifications during the years 1967–1980, Gillespie and Norman (1984) found that over 60 percent of those certified to adult courts were property offenders. Bortner (1986) conducted a four-year study of waiver trends in a large western U.S. metropolitan county. She found little or no support for the idea that transferred juveniles were singularly dangerous or violent offenders. Furthermore, Bortner noted that between 1979 and 1982, the rate of transfers had tripled, although the rate of major felonious index crimes remained fairly stable.

An examination of 583 prosecutorial waivers of sixteen- and seventeen-year-old juveniles in Florida for the period, 1981–1984, revealed findings similar to Gillespie and Norman (1984) and Bortner (1986). Bishop et al. (1989) found that most transferred juveniles were property and low-risk offenders, and not the kinds of dangerous, repeat offenders for whom waivers are arguably justified. They have explained this phenomenon by attacking the prosecutorial waiver. They maintain that this type of waiver allows prosecutors too much latitude in determining whether to initiate proceedings in juvenile or criminal courts. Since few, if any, statutory guidelines exist (in the jurisdictions they studied) to govern which cases are selected for transfer, prosecutorial decision making in this regard has been largely subjective.

These observations made by Bishop, Frazier, and Henretta are particularly insightful insofar as they help us to understand why proportionately larger numbers of property offenders are selected for transfer. In many jurisdictions there are no guidelines for prosecutors or judges to follow when deciding whether to transfer juveniles to criminal courts. Of course, the automatic transfer provision in selected states is quite clear about who qualifies for waiver. If you are sixteen or seventeen years of age, and if you have been charged with homicide, rape, or armed robbery (New York and Illinois), you will automatically be transferred to adult court for processing. You may fight the waiver and have your attorney to move to have it reversed, but the provisions for who should be transferred are clear-cut.

In most jurisdictions, however, transfers of juveniles are initiated or decided by prosecutors and judges. The subjectivity of this process is all too obvious. Particularly troublesome teenagers, not necessarily serious offenders, may be targeted for transfer by prosecutors and judges who are tired of seeing them in their courtrooms. These teenagers include habitual or persistent petty offenders who commit burglary, larceny, or who deal in illicit drugs. This group may also include habitual truants and runaways who exhibit a pattern of violation of court orders to participate in treatment programs, attend school, observe curfew, and other conditions imposed at the time of their adjudication.

Attempts to rationalize the transfer process, apart from drafting automatic waiver statutes, have been observed in some states. For instance, in 1980 Minnesota sought to codify transfer procedures to be followed by prosecutors and judges, largely on the basis of criteria including age, alleged offense, and prior record (Osbun and Rode 1984). Minnesota's attempt at juvenile court reform was designed to identify those juveniles who were presumed unfit for retention in juvenile court. However, Osbun and Rode (1984) found accurate and reliable predictive criteria to be elusive, and they eventually concluded that Minnesota's "objective criteria" were inadequate for making good transfer decisions.

All too frequently, the waiver is used merely as a convenient tool for shifting jurisdiction over certain juveniles to adult courts. Cosmetically, it appears as though juvenile courts are "getting tough" with juveniles by remanding them to criminal court. The increased use of waivers by prosecutors and judges in recent years is indicative of their response to the public outcry over perceived increases in juvenile violence in various communities. Whether or not the amount of violence among juveniles is actually increasing is academic and irrelevant. The fact is that the public perceives it to be increasing, and therefore, it must be increasing. Something must be done about it, and the waiver is a tangible manifestation of action taken by juvenile courts to deal with crime committed by juveniles.

Numbers of transfers in any jurisdiction are easily measured and counted, and transfer "trends" may be plotted as evidence of their increased use by prosecutors and judges. But as we have seen repeatedly, many juveniles entering criminal courts through the method of waiver become anonymous cases, like so many others. Criminal court prosecutors must decide whether to prosecute or not. In short, all options presented in an earlier section of this chapter are now available to transferred juveniles. These options include declined prosecution, diversion, plea bargaining, and strategic leniency from compassionate criminal court judges in the form of probation, one of several intermediate punishments, or short incarcerative terms in local jails or prisons.

JUDICIAL VIEWS ON PROCESSING JUVENILES

How do criminal court judges react to the fact of greater numbers of transferred juveniles in their courtrooms? Before responding to this question, it must be remembered that prosecutors effectively screen many of these transfer cases and nolle prosequi them. Next, many guilty pleas are elicited from transferred offenders without a formal court proceeding. Considering that less than one-half of 1 percent of all state prison inmates are under age eighteen, it would seem that the number of juvenile offenders who ultimately have their cases adjudicated in the criminal courtroom is not overwhelming.

Frankly, little is known about the personal views of criminal court judges who preside in juvenile transfer cases. Impressions gleaned from a sampling of judges in various southern jurisdictions suggest that if anything, these judges are annoyed with a significant proportion of these transfer cases, especially those involving nonviolent property crimes (Champion 1989a). Informal interviews disclose their general belief that juvenile judges should have imposed appropriate penalties for most of these property offenders, and that transferring jurisdiction over them to criminal courts accomplishes nothing more than an increasingly crowded criminal court docket. Furthermore, transferred juveniles who are convicted and incarcerated must associate with their adult counterparts in jails and prisons. Thus, some judges perceived a "conflict of interest" situation, where they were obliged to impose incarceration as a punishment on the one hand, but on the other hand they expressed disdain for a policy that would expose such youthful offenders to intimate associations with adults in prison settings.

One's youthfulness is regarded in many jurisdictions as a mitigating factor. This is favorable for juveniles when they are processed in criminal courts. However, some evidence suggests that transferred youths who go through the trial process receive no special consideration because of their youthfulness. For instance, a follow-up investigation of 206 waivers in a large metropolitan county in northern California between 1978 and 1983 revealed that for violent juveniles who had been transferred, sentences ultimately imposed by criminal court judges were considerably more severe than they would have been if adjudicated in juvenile court (Barnes et al. 1989). However, in the same research, transferred juvenile property offenders were treated with *greater leniency* than if they had been adjudicated in juvenile courts. This finding is generally consistent with what is known about the "property crime/punishment" relation pertaining to transferred juveniles, presented earlier.

While little is known about the personal views of judges, their treatment of juvenile offenders may be tracked and assessed by means of the sentences they impose. Several recent studies show that most juveniles transferred to criminal courts are seventeen and have been charged with property offenses (U.S. Department of Justice, 1988b:79; Szymanski 1989; Hamparian et al. 1982). Furthermore, over half of those juveniles who are convicted receive fines and/or probation rather than incarceration. One major reason for this is that in criminal courts, transferred juveniles are considered first-offenders, regardless of their prior juvenile records (U.S. Department of Justice 1988b:79). And when juveniles are compared with adults regarding sentencing severity on a crime-for-crime basis, juveniles either receive similar or more lenient treatment from criminal court judges. If these judges engage in disparate sentencing practices between juveniles and adults, regarding similar crimes, they seem inclined to err on the side of leniency toward juvenile offenders.

JUVENILE RIGHTS AND THE RIGHTS OF CRIMINALS, COMPARED

Until the mid-1960s, juvenile courts had a free hand in regulating the affairs of minors, primarily rooted in the doctrine of parens patriae. Whenever juveniles were apprehended by police officers for alleged infractions of the law, they were eventually turned over to juvenile authorities or taken to a "juvenile hall" for further processing. They were not advised of their right to an attorney, to have an attorney present during an interrogation, or to remain silent. They could be questioned by police at length, without parental notification or legal contact. In short, they had little, if any protection against adult constitutional rights violations on the part of law enforcement officers and others. They had no access to due process because of their status as juveniles.

When juveniles appeared before juvenile court judges, they seldom had an opportunity to rebut evidence presented against them or to test the reliability of witnesses through cross-examination. This was rationalized, at the time, by asserting that juveniles did not understand the law and had to have it interpreted for them by others, namely juvenile court judges. Subsequent investigations of the knowledge youths have of their rights seems to confirm this assertion (Lawrence 1984).

Prosecutors were seldom present in juvenile proceedings since they were nonadversarial, and juvenile court judges handled most cases informally, independently, and subjectively, depending upon the youth's needs and offense seriousness. If judges decided that secure detention would best serve the interests of justice and the welfare of the juvenile, then the youth would be placed for an indeterminate period in a secure detention facility—in many ways similar to adult prisons or jails. These decisions were seldom questioned or challenged.

One major reason for the silent acceptance of these judges' decisions was that the U.S. Supreme Court had demonstrated repeatedly that it was reluctant to intervene in the affairs of juvenile courts. In the case of *In re Gault* (discussed below), Justice Stewart typified the traditional orientation of former Supreme Courts by declaring:

The Court today uses an obscure Arizona case as a vehicle to impose upon thousands of juvenile-courts throughout the Nation restrictions that the Constitution made applicable to adversary criminal trials. I believe the Court's decision is *wholly unsound* [emphasis added] as a matter of constitutional law, and sadly unwise as a matter of judicial policy.... The inflexible restrictions that the Constitution so wisely made applicable to adversary criminal trials have no inevitable place in the proceedings of those public social agencies known as juvenile or family courts (387 U.S. at 78–79).

Thus, juvenile courts or "public social agencies" were given almost complete autonomy and authority to act in a juvenile's behalf, taking whatever action was deemed necessary. Usually, the "action deemed necessary" was closely aligned with some form of rehabilitation or had rehabilitation as a primary objective.

Because of the informality of juvenile proceedings in most jurisdictions, there were obvious abuses of judicial discretion, primarily because of the absence of consistent guidelines whereby cases could be adjudicated. Juvenile probation officers might casually recommend to judges that particular youths "ought to do a few months" in a training school or other secure detention facility, and the judge might be persuaded to adjudicate these cases accordingly.

However, several forces were at work, simultaneously, during the 1950s and 1960s that would eventually have the conjoint consequence of making juvenile courts more accountable for specific adjudications of youthful offenders. One of these forces was increased parental and public recognition of the liberal license taken by juvenile courts in administering juveniles' affairs. The abuse of judicial discretion was becoming increasingly apparent and widely known. Additionally, there was a growing disenchantment with and apathy for the rehabilitation ideal, although this disenchantment was not directed solely at juvenile courts. Rogers and Mays (1987:383) note that "disaffection during the 1960s and 1970s with the juvenile court was typical of the disenchantment then with many of society's institutions."

Regardless of the causes, several significant changes were about to be made in the juvenile justice system and the way in which youths were to be processed in future years. In this section we will examine several important rights bestowed upon juveniles by the U.S. Supreme Court during the past several decades. Delineating these rights will make clear those rights juveniles did not have until the landmark cases associated with them were concluded. Then a comparison will be made between juvenile rights and those rights that may be exercised by adults charged with crimes. However, despite sweeping juvenile reforms and major legal gains, substantial differences remain between the current rights of juveniles and adults when charged with offenses.

Kent v. United States

Regarded as the first major juvenile rights case to preface further juvenile court reforms, *Kent v. United States* (1966) established the universal precedents of (1) requiring waiver hearings before juveniles can be transferred to the jurisdiction of a criminal court (excepting legislative automatic waivers as discussed in this and other chapters, although reverse waiver hearings must be conducted at the juvenile's request); and (2) entitling juveniles to consult with counsel prior to and during such hearings.

These are the facts in the case. In 1959, Morris A. Kent, Jr., a fourteen-year-old in the District of Columbia, was apprehended as the result of several housebreakings and attempted purse snatchings. He was placed on probation in the custody of his mother. In 1961, an intruder entered the apartment of a woman, took her wallet, and raped her. Fingerprints at the crime scene were later identified as those of Morris Kent, who was fingerprinted when apprehended for housebreaking in 1959. On September 5, 1961, Kent, sixteen, was taken into custody by police, interrogated for seven hours, and admitted the offense as well as volunteering information about other housebreakings, robberies, and rapes. Although the records are unclear about when Kent's mother became aware of Kent's arrest, she did obtain counsel for Kent shortly after 2:00 P.M. the following day. She and her attorney conferred with the Social Service director of the juvenile court and learned there was a possibility Kent would be waived to criminal court. Kent's attorney advised the director of his intention to oppose the waiver.

Kent was detained in a receiving home for one week. During that period, there was no arraignment and no determination by a judicial officer of probable cause for Kent's arrest. His attorney filed a motion with the juvenile court opposing the waiver as well as a request to inspect records relating to Kent's previous offenses. Also, a psychiatric examination of Kent was arranged by Kent's attorney. Kent's attorney argued that because his client was "a victim of severe psychopathology," it would be in Kent's best interests to remain within juvenile court jurisdiction where he could receive adequate treatment in a hospital, and would be a suitable subject for rehabilitation.

Typical of juvenile court judges at the time, the juvenile judge failed to rule on any of Kent's attorney's motions. He also failed to confer with Kent's attorney and or his parents. In a somewhat arrogant manner, the juvenile judge declared that "after full investigation, I do hereby waive" jurisdiction of Kent and direct that he be "held for trial for [the alleged] offenses under the regular procedure of the U.S. District Court for the District of Columbia." He offered no findings, nor did he recite any reason for the waiver or make mention of Kent's attorney's motions. Kent was later found guilty of six counts of housebreaking by a federal jury, although the jury found him "not guilty by reason of insanity" on the rape charge. Because of District of Columbia law, it was mandatory that Kent be transferred to a mental institution until he was deemed sane. On each of the housebreaking counts, Kent's sentence was five to fifteen years, or a total of thirty to ninety years in prison. His mental institution commitment would be counted as time served against the sentence of thirty to ninety years.

By the narrowest of Supreme Court margins, Kent's conviction was reversed by a vote of 5 to 4. This is significant because it signified a subtle shift in Supreme Court sentiment relating to juvenile rights. The majority held that Kent's rights to due process and to the effective assistance of counsel were violated when he was denied a formal hearing on the waiver and his attorney's motions were ignored. It is also significant that the Supreme Court stressed the phrase, "critically important," when referring to the absence of counsel and waiver hearing respectively. In adult cases, critical stages are those that relate to the defendant's potential loss of freedoms (i.e., incarceration). Because of the *Kent* decision, waiver hearings are now critical stages. Regarding the effective assistance of counsel—this was also regarded by the Court as a "critically important" decision. They observed that "the right to representation by counsel is not a formality. It is not a grudging gesture to a ritualistic requirement. It is of the essence of justice. . . . Appointment of counsel without affording an opportunity for a hearing on a 'critically important' decision is tantamount to a denial of counsel" (383 U.S. at 561).

In re Gault

Next came *In re Gault* (1967). The *Gault* case is perhaps the most noteworthy of all landmark juvenile rights cases. Certainly it is considered the most ambitious. In a 7 to 2 vote, the U.S. Supreme Court articulated the following rights for all juveniles: (1) the right to a notice of charges; (2) the right to counsel; (3) the right to confront and cross-examine witnesses; and (4) the right to invoke the privilege against self-incrimination. The petitioner, Gault, requested the Court to rule favorably on two additional rights sought: (1) the right to a transcript of the proceedings and (2) the right to appellate review. The Court elected *not* to rule on either of these rights.

The facts in the case are that Gerald Francis Gault, a fifteen-year-old, and a friend, Ronald Lewis, were taken into custody by the Sheriff of Gila County, Arizona in the morning of June 8, 1964. At the time, Gault was on probation as the result of "being in the company of another" who had stolen a wallet from a lady's purse," a judgment entered February 25, 1964. A verbal complaint had been filed by a neighbor of Gault, Mrs. Cook, alleging that Gault had called her and made lewd and indecent remarks. [With some levity, the Supreme Court said that "It will suffice for purposes of this opinion to say that the remarks or questions put to her were of the irritatingly offensive, adolescent, sex variety" (387 U.S. at 4)]. When Gault was picked up, his mother and father were at work. Indeed, they did not learn where their son was until much later that evening. Gault was being held at the Children's Detention Home.

Gault's parents proceeded to the Home. Officer Flagg, the deputy probation officer and superintendent of the Children's Detention Home where Gault was being detained, advised Gault's parents that a hearing would be held in juvenile court at 3:00 P.M. the following day. Flagg filed a petition with the court on the hearing day, June 9. This petition was entirely formal, stating only that "said minor is under the age of 18 years, and is in need of the protection of this

Honorable Court; [and that] said minor is a delinquent minor." It prayed for a hearing and an order regarding the "care and custody of said minor." No factual basis was provided for the petition, and Gault's parents were not provided with a copy of it in advance of the hearing.

On June 9, the hearing was held, with only Gault, his mother and older brother, Probation Officers Flagg and Henderson, and the juvenile judge present. The original complainant, Mrs. Cook, was not there. No one was sworn at the hearing, no transcript was made of it, and no memorandum of the substance of the proceedings was prepared. The testimony consisted largely of allegations by Officer Flagg about Gault's behavior and prior juvenile record. A subsequent hearing was scheduled for June 15. On June 15, another hearing was held, with all above present, including Ronald Lewis and his father, and Gerald's father. What actually transpired is unknown, although there are conflicting recollections from all parties who were there. Mrs. Gault asked why Mrs. Cook was not present. Judge McGhee said, "she didn't have to be present at that hearing." Furthermore, the judge did not speak to Mrs. Cook or communicate with her at any time. Flagg spoke with her once, by telephone on June 9. Officially, the charge against Gault was "lewd phone calls." When the hearing was concluded, the judge committed Gault as a juvenile delinquent to the Arizona State Industrial School "for a period of his minority" [until age 21].[2]

A habeas corpus hearing was held on August 17, and Judge McGhee was cross-examined regarding his actions. After hemming and hawing, the judge declared that Gault had "disturbed the peace" and was "habitually involved in immoral matters." Regarding the judge's reference to Gault's alleged "habitual immoral" behavior, the judge made vague references to an incident two years earlier when Gault had been accused of stealing someone's baseball glove and had lied to police by denying that he had taken it. The judge also recalled, again vaguely, that Gault had testified some months earlier about making "silly calls, or funny calls, or something like that."

After exhausting their appeals in Arizona state courts, the Gaults appealed to the U.S. Supreme Court. The Court was appalled that Gault's case had been handled in such a cavalier and unconstitutional manner. They reversed the Arizona Supreme Court, holding that Gault did, indeed, have the right to an attorney, the right to confront his accuser (Mrs. Cook) and to cross-examine her, the right of protection against self-incrimination, and the right to have notice of the charges filed against him. Perhaps Justice Hugo L. Black summed up the current juvenile court situation in the United States when he said, "This holding strikes a well-nigh fatal blow to much that is *unique* [*emphasis added*] about the juvenile courts in this Nation."

In re Winship

Winship was a relatively simple case compared with *Gault*. However, it set an important precedent in juvenile courts relating to the standard of proof used in establishing defendant guilt. The U.S. Supreme Court held that "beyond a reasonable doubt," a standard ordinarily used in adult criminal courts, was henceforth to be used by juvenile court judges and others in establishing a youth's delinquency. Formerly, the standard used was the civil application of "preponderance of the evidence."

The facts relating to *Winship* are that Samuel Winship was a twelve-year-old charged with larceny in New York City. He purportedly entered a locker and stole $112 from a woman's pocketbook. Under Section 712 of the New York Family Court Act, a juvenile delinquent was defined as "a person over seven and less than sixteen years of age who does any act, which, if done by an adult, would constitute a crime." Interestingly, the juvenile judge in the case acknowledged that the proof to be presented by the prosecution might be insufficient to establish the guilt of Winship beyond a reasonable doubt, although he did indicate that the New York Family Court Act provided that "any determination at the conclusion of [an adjudicatory hearing] that a [juvenile] did an act or acts must be based on a preponderance of the evidence" standard (397 U.S. at 360). Winship was adjudicated as a delinquent and ordered to a training school for eighteen months, subject to annual extensions of his commitment until his eighteenth birthday. Appeals to New York courts were unsuccessful.

The U.S. Supreme Court eventually heard Winship's case and, in a 6 to 3 vote, reversed the New York Family Court ruling. A statement by Justice Brennan succinctly states the case for the "beyond a reasonable doubt" standard:

In sum, the constitutional safeguard of proof beyond a reasonable doubt is as much required during the adjudicatory stage of a delinquency proceeding as are those constitutional safeguards applied in *Gault*—notice of charges, right to counsel, the rights of confrontation and examination, and the privilege of self-incrimination. We therefore hold, in agreement with Chief Justice Fuld in dissent in the Court of Appeals, that where a 12-year-old child is charged with an act of stealing which renders him liable to confinement for as long as six years, then, as a matter of due process... the case against him must be proved beyond a reasonable doubt (397 U.S. at 368).

McKeiver v. Pennsylvania

The *McKeiver* case was important because the U.S. Supreme Court held that juveniles are not entitled to a jury trial as a matter of right. The facts are that in May 1968, Joseph McKeiver, age sixteen, was charged with robbery, larceny, and receiving stolen goods. Although he was represented by counsel at his adjudicatory hearing and requested a trial by jury to ascertain his guilt or innocence, Judge Theodore S. Gutowicz of the Court of Common Pleas, Family Division, Juvenile Branch, of Philadelphia, Pennsylvania denied the request. McKeiver was subsequently adjudicated delinquent. On appeal to the U.S. Supreme Court, McKeiver's adjudication was upheld. Again (of interest to criminal justice analysts), the remarks of a U.S. Supreme Court Justice are insightful. Justice Harry A. Blackmun indicated: "If the formalities of the criminal adjudicative process are to be superimposed upon the juvenile court system, there is little need for its separate existence. Perhaps that ultimate disillusionment will come one day, but for the moment, we are disinclined to give impetus to it" (403 U.S. at 551).

Throughout the opinion delivered in the *McKeiver* case, it is apparent that the Supreme Court was sensitive to the problems associated with juvenile court procedures. Since criminal courts were already bogged down with formalities and lengthy protocol that frequently led to excessive court delays, it was not unreasonable for the Court to rule against subjecting juvenile courts to such formalities. But we must recognize that in this instance, the Court merely ruled that it is not the constitutional right of juveniles to have a jury trial upon their request. This proclamation had no effect on individual states that wished to enact or preserve such a method of adjudicating delinquent juveniles. Therefore, about one-fourth of the states today have legislative provisions for jury trials in juvenile courts.

Breed v. Jones

In *Breed v. Jones* (1975), the significant constitutional issue of "double jeopardy" was raised. The U.S. Supreme Court concluded that after a juvenile has been adjudicated delinquent on specific charges, those same charges may not be alleged subsequently in criminal courts through transfers or waivers.

The facts of the case are that on February 8, 1971 in Los Angeles, California, Gary Steven Jones, seventeen years old, was armed with a deadly weapon and allegedly committed robbery. Jones was subsequently apprehended and an adjudicatory hearing was held on March 1. After testimony was taken from Jones and witnesses, the Juvenile Court found that the allegations were true and sustained the petition. A dispositional hearing date was set for March 15. At that time, Jones was declared "not . . . amenable to the care, treatment and training program available through the facilities of the juvenile court" under a California statute. Jones then was transferred by judicial waiver to a California criminal court to be tried as an adult. In a later criminal trial, Jones was convicted of robbery and committed for an indeterminate period to the California Youth Authority. The California Supreme Court upheld the conviction.

When Jones appealed the decision in 1971, the U.S. Supreme Court reversed the robbery conviction. Chief Justice Warren Burger delivered the Court opinion: "We hold that the prosecution of [Jones] in Superior Court, after an adjudicatory proceeding in Juvenile Court, violated the Double Jeopardy Clause of the Fifth Amendment, as applied to the States through the Fourteenth Amendment." The Court ordered Jones's release outright or a remand to juvenile court for disposition. In a lengthy opinion, Justice Burger targeted double jeopardy as (1) being adjudicated as delinquent on specific charges in a juvenile court, and (2) subsequently being tried and convicted on those same charges in criminal court. Within the context of "fundamental fairness," such action could not be tolerated.

Schall v. Martin

In the *Schall v. Martin* (1984) case, the U.S. Supreme Court issued juveniles a minor setback regarding the state's right to hold them in preventive detention pending a subsequent adjudication. The Court said that the preventive detention of juveniles by states is constitu-tional, if judges perceive these youths to pose a danger to the com-munity or an otherwise serious risk if released before an adjudicatory hearing. This decision was significant, in part, because many experts advocated the separation of juveniles and adults in jails—the facilities most often used for preventive detention. Also, the preventive de-tention of adults was not ordinarily practiced at that time.[3]

The facts are that fourteen-year-old Gregory Martin was arrested at 11:30 P.M. on December 13, 1977 in New York City. He was charged with first-degree robbery, second-degree assault, and criminal pos-session of a weapon. Martin lied to police at the time, giving a false name and address. Between the time of his arrest and December 29 when a fact-finding hearing was held, Martin was detained (a total of 15 days). His detention was based largely on the false information he had supplied to police and the seriousness of the charges pending against him. Subsequently, he was adjudicated delinquent and placed on two years' probation. Later, his attorney filed an appeal, contesting his preventive detention as violative of the Due Process Clause of the Fourteenth Amendment. The U.S. Supreme Court eventually heard the case and upheld the detention as constitutional.

Each of these cases represents attempts by juveniles to secure rights ordinarily extended to adults. Given these cases, juveniles have fared well with the U.S. Supreme Court in past years. However, there are still major differences between the juvenile justice system and the criminal justice system and how offenders of different ages are pro-cessed. Rogers and Mays (1987:364–365) have highlighted some of the major differences between criminal and juvenile courts in Table 5.1.

SUMMARY

There are trial courts in all state and federal jurisdictions. These courts may have exclusively criminal jurisdiction, or they may have general jurisdiction to hear and decide a broad range of cases—including civil litigation. Serious criminal cases, especially felonies, are heard in courts of record—where a transcript, tape-recording, or other reproduction is made of the proceedings. Thus, if convicted offenders wish to appeal to higher courts regarding verdicts or jury outcomes, they can reconstruct what transpired. Different types of court organization typify state courts and exhibit considerable diversity. The federal district court is the major trial court for the federal government where serious crimes are alleged.

The major goal of criminal courts is to provide objective and impartial adversarial forums within which cases may be heard and adjudicated. They are guided in their actions by rules of criminal procedure applicable to specific state or federal jurisdictions. Certain rules that regulate the admissibility of evidence and testimony of witnesses are also followed. Most convictions in criminal courts are secured through plea bargaining. Most of the cases that eventually do come to trial result in guilty verdicts.

In recent years, greater numbers of serious juvenile offenders have been transferred to the jurisdiction of criminal courts. While the primary intent of such waivers is to expose these juveniles to a stricter, harsher, and broader range of punishments, including the death penalty, the true punishments meted out to transferred juveniles are not always as severe as the punishments they may have received in family or juvenile courts.

For many years, juvenile courts have been dominated by a rehabilitative philosophy, and parens patriae has operated to provide juvenile court judges with great discretion in adjudicating cases. In recent years, however, several important landmark juvenile rights cases have been decided by the U.S. Supreme Court. While the Supreme Court was reluctant for many years to intervene in the affairs of family or juvenile courts, the 1960s prefaced major reforms pertaining to juvenile rights. Major cases include *Kent v. United States* (1966), *In re Gault* (1967), and *In re Winship* (1970) where juveniles were granted the right to a waiver hearing and presence of an attorney before transfers could occur (with exceptions), the right to counsel generally, notice of charges, the right against self-incrimination, the right to cross-examine witnesses, and the establishment of "beyond a reasonable doubt" as the standard of proof comparable to the standard used in criminal court proceedings. While most juvenile courts do not ordinarily grant juveniles the right to a trial by jury, this provision exists legislatively in at least twelve states. Also, juveniles have the right against double jeopardy stemming from the same charges in both juvenile and criminal courts. Juveniles may be preventatively detained, however.

In the opinion of certain critics, juvenile courts are not tough

Table 5.1

A comparison of juvenile courts and criminal courts

Criminal Courts	Juvenile Courts
1. The proceedings are adversary: the state against (versus) the accused.	1. The proceedings are governed by the principles of *parens patriae* and in *loco patentis:* that is , the state serves as the guardian of the child and in place of the natural parents.
2. Charges against the accused are formulated through an indictment by a grand jury or on information filed by a prosecuting attorney as outlined in the criminal code.	2. A petition is filed on behalf of or in the interest of the child. It specifies certain allegations involving behavior covered by the children's code.
3. While awaiting trial, the person charged may be released on his or her own recognizance (i.e., reputation or trust) or by posting bond. Pretrial detention in jail is common.	3. Most commonly children remain with their parents while awaiting their juvenile court hearing. When detention is deemed necessary, the child may be held in a specialized facility, ideally seperated by sight and sound from adult offenders.
4. Although plea bargining is common, the prosecution and defense are carried out by seperate distinctive parties. A prosecutor presents the state's case confronting an opposing attroney employed by the defendant or assigned by the court to those unable to afford counsel.	4. Until *Gault* prosecution attorneys seldom participate, and a defense counsel is rarely used. The juvenile probation officer is assumed capable of representing the mutual interests of the child, the family, and the community, including the victim The presiding judge is assumed capable of protecting the collective welfare of all parties.
5. There is a trial on a specific charge to determine guilt or innocence, or the defendant pleads guilty to the charge. The accused has the right to a jury trial	5. Originally a hearing was held simultaneously sustaining or disaffirming the allegations of the petition and establishing the child's need for continued state intervention. Juries are rarely used. When deemed essential, the case may be transferred under special circumstances to an adult court.
6. The trial is public and formal, with the records open to the media. Details are entered into the files of the Federal Bureau of Investigation (the "rap sheet").	6. The hearing is private and informal, perhaps being held in the judge's chambers. The child's name and records are confidential; neither photographs or fingerprints are allowed. Exceptions, allowed by the court, are rare.
7. The trial is conducted under strict rules of evidence, with the standard test being "proof beyond a resonable doubt." The defendant's life history is deemed irrelevant and except under special circumstances is excluded from the trial.	7. In juvenile court hearings, both social and legal information are utilized. It is common for the former to be more relevant than the latter in determing to state's continuing role in the case.

Table 5.1 (continued)

Criminal Courts	Juvenile Courts
8. To the extent that the court asks for a social investigation, it comes after the determination of guilt and before sentencing. It is called a presentence investigation ("PSI") or a presentence report ("PSR"). These are completed by members of an adult probation and parole officers.	8. A social investigation or social case history is basic. It is completed by the juvenile probation officer operating more as a social worker than as an officer of the law. The spirit is one of caring and helping, and seeking to find solutions by finding cause and making an appropriate diagnosis.
9. A sentence, within the limits set by law, is pronounced. Consistent with a punitive philosophy, the sentence generally is a fine, a period of incarceration in jail or in prison, or both. Probation may be allowable by law.	9. The court's disposition is primarily concerned with the child's need for rehabilitation and treatment. Constructive remedies are sought, with every effort being made to keep the child at home with the family. Incarceration is a last resort.

Source: Joseph W. Rogers and G. Larry Mays, *Juvenile Delinquency and Juvenile Justice*. Englewood Cliffs, NJ: Prentice-Hall, 1987, pp. 364-65. Reprinted with permission.

enough on the juveniles who are processed by them. The "get tough" movement has led to substantial juvenile court reforms, including greater use of the transfer or waiver. The primary purpose of increasing the use of such waivers is to make it possible for more severe punishments to be imposed on convicted juveniles compared with the punishment options within the purview of juvenile court judges. However, leniency at all stages, from the prosecution to the judiciary, is typical of how juvenile offenders generally fare in the adult system. Indications are that transfers are used primarily as a cosmetic, to give the appearance of greater toughness in dealing with juvenile offenders.

NOTES

1. It is beyond the scope of this book to provide substantial details of court structure and organization. Most introductory books on criminal justice or criminal law furnish ample descriptions of court procedures and pro-

cesses, as well as highlight distinctions between different types of courts. The present discussion will be limited to general court phenomena as they relate to the constitutional rights of adult and juvenile defendants.

2. If an adult had made an obscene telephone call, he would have received a fifty-dollar fine and no more than sixty days in jail. In Gerald Gault's case, he was facing nearly six years in a juvenile prison for the same offense.

3. Since then, the preventive detention of adults who are deemed to pose societal risks has been upheld by the U.S. Supreme Court in *United States v. Salerno* (1987).

CHAPTER 6

Juvenile Transfer Trends: A Look Ahead

To ask about the future of juvenile transfers is to ask about the future of the juvenile court, and the juvenile justice system itself. However, some trends extend beyond the juvenile justice system and deal with general judicial processes. This chapter will review some of the prevailing trends in juvenile justice and project where these trends will take juvenile courts generally, and where, specifically, transfers may be heading.

CHANGES IN AMERICAN JUDICIAL PROCESSES

The twentieth century has witnessed major changes in the organization and operation of American courts. Federal and state courts have been subjected to continuing efforts to reform them (Glick 1983). This section will explore some of the elements of American court reform, and how these efforts will impact on juvenile court operations.

Court Unification

One of the key thrusts of the court reform movement has been court unification. Three elements characterize the court unification movement: simplified court structure, centralized rule making, and statewide financing (Neubauer 1988). In terms of impact on juvenile court processes, the most important element of the court unification movement is a simplified court structure. In simplest terms this means that states move away from specialized juvenile courts dealing with a relatively narrow range of delinquency, dependency, and neglect cases to courts of general jurisdiction handling criminal and civil matters for adults and juveniles (Rubin 1989:113–14). Within such a structure, however, judges may specialize, and certain judges may be designated to hear juvenile cases. The key tenet for court unification is specialized judges, not specialized courts. Conversely, unified courts may designate family division judges, rotate judges between hearing adult and juvenile cases, or all judges may have juvenile cases assigned to their caseloads.

It should be recognized, however, that not everyone is enthusiastic about the joining of juvenile and adult adjudications in one court. In fact, the President's Commission on Law Enforcement and Administration of Justice (1967) explicitly recommended not eliminating juvenile courts and not merging them with adult criminal courts. Their report noted: "As trying as are the problems of the juvenile courts, the problems of the criminal courts, particularly those of the lower courts that would fall heir to much of the juvenile court jurisdiction, are even graver; and the ideal of separate treatment of children is still worth pursuing."

One alternative to a fully unified court system, and one chosen by a number of states during the 1960s and 1970s, is the *family court*. The National Advisory Committee for Criminal Justice Standards and Goals (1976) made the first recommendation for the creation of a family court. This recommendation was repeated by the National Advisory Committee for Juvenile Justice and Delinquency Prevention (1980). This group, in its Standards 3.12 and 3.121, suggested that the family court should be a division of the highest state court of general trial jurisdiction (National Advisory Committee 1980:266). The principal idea behind a family court is that the child cannot be dealt with in isolation from the family. Thus, family courts assume broad jurisdiction over juvenile cases, domestic relations (divorces and custody suits), paternity suits, and many probate matters. The National Advisory Committee (1980:260) recommended that the family court have delinquency jurisdiction over children between the ages of ten and eighteen, and that delinquency jurisdiction be fairly narrowly drawn, essentially confined to offenses that would be misdemeanors or felonies for adults (1980:247). Standard 3.112 also recommended that while the family court retain status offense jurisdiction, it should be limited to habitual truancy, repeated absences from home for more than 24 hours, repeated disregard for parental authority, and acts of delinquency committed by children under the age of ten (1980:249).

For some states the political prospects of reorganizing the entire court apparatus seem overwhelming. Short of this, however, one possible compromise is the creation of a family court.

Judges' Qualifications

In some cases, states have considered juvenile courts as one of the courts of limited jurisdiction. This has meant that juvenile courts did not conduct jury trials, did not produce verbatim transcripts of proceedings, and required appeals to go *de novo* to the courts of general trial jurisdiction. A number of observers have suggested that the courts of inferior jurisdiction are so designated because of the quality of justice they dispense (Robertson 1974). One of the hallmarks of courts of limited jurisdiction in the United States has been the use of judges not required to be licensed attorneys. The President's Commission (1967:80) found in a study conducted at the time of the *Gault* decision that half of the juvenile judges "had no undergraduate degree; a fifth had received no college education at all; a fifth were not members of the bar." Because many people considered this to be a deplorable situation, the National Advisory Committee (1980:268) recommended that family court judges should not only be attorneys, but individuals interested in working with juveniles who have problems. A general trend of American courts, including juvenile courts, is the movement away from lay (i.e., nonlawyer) judges to judges who are licensed attorneys (Glick 1983). Ideally, as suggested by the National Advisory Committee (1980), juvenile courts would not only have lawyer-judges, but judges with experience, training, and the inclination to work in juvenile court.

More Formalized Procedures

Juvenile courts are characterized by increasingly formal proceedings. This situation has been brought about by the frequent presence of attorneys for both sides, and the increasing application of rules of procedure, jury trials in some states, and a generally adversarial atmosphere. The "due process revolution" of the late 1960s and early 1970s has created a juvenile court with a legal environment much like adult criminal courts, and unlike the ideal of the original juvenile court.

One manifestation of more formal, adultlike procedures is the use of determinate sentencing and sentencing and sentencing guidelines (Schneider 1984b). These changes in sentencing procedures demonstrate a general dissatisfaction with indeterminate sentencing, parole, and the rehabilitative philosophy associated with them (Mays 1989; for an extended discussion of sentencing guidelines, see Champion 1989b). Sentencing guidelines are designed to do a number of things, depending on one's point of view: constrain the discretion of judges, assist judges in dispositional decisions, remove the disparity and uncertainty of parole decision making, and make dispositions more uniform and proportionate to the offense. Schneider (1984b), in an evaluation of Washington State's juvenile sentencing guidelines, found that the more punitive orientation of the justice model (exemplified through the use of sentencing guidelines) apparently has had little impact on recidivism rates. Nevertheless, more formalized procedures seem to be a clear trend in juvenile procedures.

TRENDS IN JUVENILE TRANSFERS

While the previous sections examined some of the general changes in juvenile court procedures, this section will explore the changes that have occurred and are occurring, specifically in transfer procedures. These trends may be a reflection of the diminished significance of the juvenile court as a separate entity. They may also be a reflection of the kinds of adaptive changes that are necessary to keep the juvenile court a viable, distinct judicial institution (Bortner 1986). In other words, increasing the number of juveniles transferred to adult court may be the type of adaptive response necessary for the juvenile court to survive into its second century of existence. It seems apparent to many observers that a number of the trends related to juvenile transfers are attempts to establish, or perhaps regain, credibility for the juvenile court and the juvenile justice system in dealing with serious offenders.

Selective Certification

Selective certification for juveniles, similar to selective incapacitation for adults, implies two things. First, there is a special, separate, and unique group of juveniles who deserve transfer to adult criminal courts. These offenders are not appropriate for juvenile court dispositions and they are deserving of the harsh penalties potentially awaiting those convicted in adult courts. Second, we can correctly identify or diagnose those deserving of such treatment with some degree of certainty. This further implies that we will not misdiagnose those who are not deserving of such handling. As with selective incapacitation, however, both assumptions may be more myth than reality.

For example, most predictive instruments employed in criminal justice (or merely experimented with) have notoriously poor performance. Unfortunately, the best prediction often is *post hoc* in nature, and hindsight makes an unsatisfying basis for a future-oriented policy. We become most aware of persistent juvenile offenders (or adult "career criminals") at the point when their offense levels start to diminish. There has been demonstrable evidence that many juvenile offenders "mature out" of criminal offending at the time when they would fall under criminal court jurisdiction. It is not simply that many of these youngsters "graduate" to criminal court, many simply stop committing offenses or at least get good enough to avoid getting caught.

Therefore, rather than relying on predictions of future behavior, many states have sought to apply selective certifications to certain categories of offenses (e.g., homicides, rapes, or armed robberies), or to those juveniles who previously have been *adjudicated* for a certain number of delinquent offenses—typically two or three (Szymanski 1989). Merely being arrested for these offenses or being petitioned to the juvenile court is not sufficient. There must be actual delinquency adjudications.

Selective certifications, unlike automatic transfers, still require motions from the state and decisions by the judge. What they provide however, is legislative guidance on when transfers are most appropriate. Thus, selective certifications do not remove cases from juvenile court jurisdiction, as automatic transfers would, but instead they help to preserve the integrity of the court's jurisdiction while responding to public pressures to be more punitive with certain juvenile offenders (Bortner 1986).

Older Juveniles and Transfers

It should surprise no one that older juveniles are those most likely to be transferred to adult courts, almost irrespective of the offenses committed. In fact, Nimick et al. (1986) note in a study of 2,335 transfers that 69.1 percent of those remanded to criminal court were seventeen years old. This was followed by 20.1 percent of sixteen-year-olds. Very few youths (4.5 percent) under the age of sixteen are transferred, primarily because of the age-offense restrictions in many states. Speirs (1989) further illustrates this point by noting that older youths (aged sixteen and seventeen) are disproportionately represented in juvenile court violence cases, accounting for 52 percent of the violence referrals. Of those aged sixteen and seventeen who were charged with violent offenses (homicide, violent sexual offenses, robbery, and aggravated assault) in a recent federal study, 59 percent were transferred to adult courts, placed in a residential facility, or placed on formal probation (Speirs 1989).

Clearly, age—especially when combined with offense seriousness—is a major factor in jurisdictional waiver decision making. However, as Feld (1987b) maintains, relying on age as the principal factor in the decision to transfer a juvenile may result in a misplaced confidence in adult courts' willingness or ability to punish young offenders. As noted previously, Feld (1987b) has found what could be termed a "halo effect" that follows not only sixteen- and seventeen-year-olds into adult court, but which applies to many offenders who are eighteen, nineteen, and twenty as well.

There are several policy options appropriate for older juvenile offenders, depending on the ultimate policy objective society may be trying to achieve. First, states with eighteen years of age as the maximum age limit of court jurisdiction can follow the lead of those states that have lowered the upper age limit to sixteen or seventeen. A variation on this is employed by Oklahoma, which uses a system of "reverse certification" where older juveniles are presumed fit for trial in adult courts unless they apply for and receive juvenile court jurisdiction over them (Cornish 1982, see also Drowns and Hess 1990:233).

Second, states that desire a more punitive response might employ the opposite strategy: they might raise the juvenile court's upper age limit to nineteen, twenty, or even twenty-one. For these young adults punishment becomes a very real possibility in a court where many offenders are only fourteen or fifteen. Compared with younger offenders, these older, but still youthful, offenders are more likely to receive some punishment (especially incarceration) and more severe sanctions than they would receive in most adult courts. Nimick et al. (1986:6) examined nine states with extended juvenile court age jurisdictions: Arizona, Iowa, and Tennessee (eighteen and nineteen years of age); Kansas, Mississippi, Pennsylvania, and Virginia (twenty and twenty-one years of age); and California and Hawaii (over twenty-one years of age). Their conclusion was

Those courts with extended jurisdiction to only the eighteenth or nineteenth birthday were more than twice as likely to waive a case than were courts which could have jurisdiction over youth until their twenty-first birthday and five times as likely as those courts with the ability to retain jurisdiction past the twenty-first birthday (Nimick et al. 1986:6).

In simplest terms, expanded age jurisdiction was associated with a diminished likelihood to invoke waivers. Therefore, while raising the upper jurisdiction age is counter-intuitive, it can be demonstrably effective.

A third alternative is to do away with separate juvenile and adult courts. In this way, juvenile offenders would not be viewed as violators occupying a narrow age threshold. Rather, they would be viewed in the context of the whole age continuum. Such an approach, already employed in states with fully unified courts, allows different judges access to a unified record-keeping system. Therefore, in those cases where it is relevant, an offender's record could be tracked from juvenile dispositions through adult dispositions. Youngsters would not be "reborn" simply by turning eighteen.

Rubin (1989) provides a number of alternatives to allow juvenile courts to retain jurisdiction over youngsters rather than remanding them to criminal court jurisdiction. All of these alternatives imply three things: closer scrutiny of adjudicated offenders, alternatives to the traditional ways of doing things, and (undoubtedly) greater expenditures of money. The eight alternatives proposed by Rubin (1989:135–36) include:

1. intensive probation supervision;
2. expanded work programs;
3. special schooling programs;
4. full-day school and work programs;
5. school combined with adventure programs;
6. short-term secure residential placements;
7. specialized foster homes combined with an alternative school; and
8. long-term residential programs.

These dispositions are designed to provide alternatives to the traditional probation/incarceration/transfer choices facing ' juvenile judges and other juvenile justice officials.

Male and Female Comparisons and Tends

Delinquency, as a social concept, is overwhelmingly a male phenomenon. For example, the figures for all arrests, adults and juveniles—indicate that only 17 percent involve females, and females account for only 20 percent of the juveniles under correctional supervision (U.S. Department of Justice 1988b:46). Additionally, the Bureau of Justice Statistics (1989:37) points out the fact that between 1975 and 1984 total male admissions to juvenile facilities declined by 6 percent (from 697,897 to 628,766). During the same time period, however, female admissions declined 21 percent (from 185,211 to 145,703).

In 1984, males were charged in 81 percent of the delinquency cases, and by 1985 that number had increased to 85 percent (Office of Juvenile Justice and Delinquency Prevention 1987, 1989). When comparing youth at risk, the male delinquency rate was more than five times the female rate (OJJDP 1989:8).

Generally, three conclusions can be reached about the relationship between delinquency and gender. First, males commit more of the serious (violent, personal) offenses than do females. Second, males as a group have more extensive offense histories than do females. And third, in terms of treatment, part of the disparity may be explained by the juvenile court's paternalistic handling of female offenders.

The question remaining is to what extent do gender factors influence transfer decisions? Speirs (1989) gives us a glimpse of some possible effects of gender. He notes, for example, that violent offense referral rates to juvenile courts are seven times greater for males than for females (88 percent of all violent youthful offenders were males). In terms of referrals for violent crimes, white females had the lowest referral rates, followed by nonwhite females, white males, and nonwhite males. In all likelihood, these relationships would hold true for cases transferred to adult courts.

IMPLICATIONS OF TRANSFERS FOR THE CRIMINAL JUSTICE SYSTEM

If juvenile cases are increasingly going to be waived to adult courts, or if the juvenile court is to be eliminated as a separate entity, then the criminal justice system is going to be faced with managing not only a bigger caseload, but a different one. This section will examine four possible consequences for the criminal justice system when faced with the prospect of adjudicating adolescent offenders.

The first implication for the criminal justice system is that adult courts will have larger caseloads with few, if any, additional resources. Adult courts are already facing large numbers of criminal offenders, with an insufficient number of prosecutors, judges, courtrooms, and dispositional resources such as probation officers, and bed space in correctional facilities. The addition of nearly half a million juvenile cases (in 1985 juvenile courts in the United States disposed of approximately 534,000 juvenile cases) (OJJDP 1989:5) would have an immeasurable effect on adult courts. Some of these cases are already handled in courts with both juvenile and adult jurisdictions, so the absolute increase would be less than half a million. However, if only half that number of cases was added to adult court caseloads, the impact would be overwhelming for many criminal courts. Case processing could literally come to a standstill, as a result of the inundation. Therefore, when considering the impact on the criminal justice system, court caseloads should be one of the first factors considered—and the possibility of catastrophic consequences cannot be discounted.

Second, not only would the criminal justice system be dealing with more cases, it also would be faced with resolving more difficult social issues. Often, in the case of adult criminal defendants, little consideration is given to making this individual a better person when the judge imposes sentencing. With juveniles there always seems to be hope for redemption or restoration. Thus, the juvenile justice system's traditional concern for rehabilitation persists, even in criminal courts. The past few decades have witnessed philosophies such as retribution, incapacitation, and deterrence controlling many of the changes in correctional policies in the United States. When dealing with adults it seems we have been willing to settle for something other than rehabilitation as our guiding principle (however, see Cullen and Gilbert 1982). For juveniles, the issue is not merely what is wrong with this particular child as a fully formed, carefully reasoning individual, but what is wrong with the child given the complex social milieu in which the child is placed. In all likelihood, adult courts will not have the time, resources, or inclination to decide these kinds of questions in regard to juvenile offenders. In all fairness, though, it is likely that juvenile courts are not doing a particularly good job at this either. The central question would seem to be, Which system will strive to provide justice for juvenile offenders, and meet their social needs?

Given the first two implications for the criminal justice system, the third likely outcome is that juvenile cases will be assigned a low priority compared to adult cases. Many states with combined adult and juvenile correctional systems can attest to the fact that juveniles typically receive not only the lowest funding priorities but, in effect, they receive the system's leftovers. Adults take first place in a mixed system for two reasons: they are more numerous, and they are more serious offenders. Ironically, most justice system officials view adult offenders as less tractable than juveniles, and therefore not as receptive to treatment, and less cost effective in terms of investment.

If juvenile cases are going to be transferred to the adult courts at increasing rates, and if criminal courts are to provide meaningful dispositions, careful case-screening procedures will have to be instituted. In most jurisdictions case screening is accomplished at one of two stages: at the point of initial investigation by the police, or at the initiation of prosecution by the prosecuting attorney. A review of most of the criminal justice literature on case screening indicates that many police departments have no routine case-screening mechanisms and that only the largest prosecuting attorney's offices engage in thorough and meaningful case reviews.

For juvenile cases transferred to adult courts, some apparatus—perhaps located in the prosecuting attorney's office or a combination prosecutor/probation system—will have to be established. This case screening mechanism will have to establish three factors: legal sufficiency of the case, the mitigating or aggravating social factors that must be taken into account, and the desirability of prosecution (i.e., prosecutorial prioritization). If such a system is established, criminal courts will have in place a scheme to allow them to maximize their meager adjudicative resources. The outcome may be an increase in the number of cases resulting in nolle prosequis or cases being returned to the juvenile courts for adjudication by the criminal courts.

A final implication for the criminal justice system involves the disposition of juveniles convicted of adult crimes. In simplest terms, what will be done with juveniles transferred to adult courts and subsequently convicted of crimes? Will they be placed in adult correctional facilities? Does the state have transitional facilities for offenders who are no longer juveniles, but who really are not yet adults? Should such facilities for "youthful offenders" be established? Should private contractors establish facilities if they are needed in states which show no inclination to establish such public facilities?

Speirs (1988) gives an overview of a private correctional program for "chronic, serious offenders." This program, the Paint Creek Youth Center in Ohio, is designed as a dispositional alternative to transferring juveniles into the adult system. This approach, and other public and private correctional programs like it, may hold the key for the whole issue of juvenile transfers. As we indicated early in this book, much of the impetus for juvenile transfers is based on the assumption that certain juvenile offenders are not appropriately retained in the juvenile justice system. The assumption is, because of the seriousness of their offenses or the persistence of their offense histories, these youngsters could be better handled (punished) in the criminal justice system. Therefore, what may be lacking is not a judicial mechanism such as waiver of jurisdiction, but dispositional alternatives such as intensive probation supervision, small and intensive housing arrangements, and short-term intensive correctional programs like some of the so-called "boot camp" programs (Rubin 1989:135–36). Most of these correctional dispositions fall into what has come to be called "intermediate punishments." These are programs between traditional probation and secure incarceration.

A final caveat must be offered concerning the expansion of correctional options for the most serious and persistent juvenile offenders. Two states, Massachusetts and Texas, have provided valuable lessons about how juvenile offenders should and should not be handled. In the 1960s Jerome Miller was responsible for what many have called the Massachusetts "experiment" with massive deinstitutionalization of juvenile offenders (Coates et al. 1978). This deinstitutionalization effort was not an experiment at all. It resulted from Miller's frustration with attempting to reform Massachusetts' juvenile corrections apparatus, which traditionally had relied heavily on secure detention of adjudicated delinquents. Nevertheless, Massachusetts showed that a move away from reliance on institutionalization—what easily can be characterized as a punitive philosophy—cannot be successful for long without some types of alternatives to secure incarceration (McCord and Sanchez 1983).

The example provided by Texas comes from the case of *Morales v. Turman* (1977). In this case, the federal district court ruled that the Texas Youth Council would have to undertake extensive changes in its training schools based on the issue of a right to treatment. The Fifth Circuit Court of Appeals sent the case back to the district court in a dispute over hearing procedures. The Supreme Court reversed the decision of the circuit court, and the stage was set for wideranging, court-ordered reforms of the state training schools in Texas (Bartollas 1990:476–77; Davis 1980:6–25; Miller et al. 1985).

In reality, litigation has furnished two mandates for state juvenile correctional systems. First, it has provided that reasonable standards relating to conditions of confinements must be maintained (for a general discussion of prison litigation see Alpert et al. 1984; Fairchild 1984; Huff and Alpert 1982; Mays and Taggart 1985). Simply put, states must operate safe, humane, constitutional correctional facilities for all convicted offenders—especially juveniles.

Second, although it has not been resolved, the right to treatment issue has been raised by the courts in regard to juvenile inmates (Rubin 1989:136). The issue of a "right" to treatment was originally articulated in the mental health field. The position taken by the federal courts was that involuntary psychiatric commitments were predicated on the provision of treatment services. Thus, states had two choices: provide treatment, or release persons confined for mental health reasons. Extending the right to treatment to juvenile correctional facilities, the courts have said that the "juvenile court exists to provide rehabilitative treatment for youths in trouble and to afford them the same kind of treatment they would receive in the family setting" (Davis 1980:6–26). One of the key cases in this area is *Inmates v. Affleck* (1972). In this case, the district court observed that "Society has bargained with these juveniles and it should be an honest bargain. They have been confined through a process offering them fewer protections than adults have; they may not now be treated worse than the adult inmates are."

SUMMARY

When dealing with the issue of juvenile transfers, serious offenders, or delinquents in general, the question is not *whether* we will do something, but *what* we will do. It seems unlikely that criminal justice and crimnology scholars, and public policy decision makers can do nothing. The public seems unwilling to settle for a policy of "do nothing." Besides, as Hackler (1978) points out, there always seems to be a "need to do something" about social problems, no matter how intractable they may be.

In the case of juvenile transfers, however, we seem to be faced with resolving two dilemmas: have we been doing *nothing*, or have we been doing the *wrong* thing? Some concluding observations may cast a light on these two concerns.

First, due process has become a very real part of the world of the juvenile court. Due process protections articulated in cases such as

Kent, Gault, Winship and *Breed v. Jones* have become a regularized part of most juvenile court processes. The result, however, has been a more adversarial system, at times scarcely distinguishable from the adult criminal justice system.

Second, as a consequence of this, there has been the development of a number of policy initiatives relating to the diversion of less serious offenders from the juvenile justice system. We must ask if a consequence of the time, effort, energy, and money spent on diverting status and other minor offenders in the juvenile system is that serious offenders have been somewhat ignored or shunted to the adult criminal justice system. With such policy thrusts, status offenders have largely dropped out of the formal juvenile justice system, although they regularly reappear in the informal, private system of diversion programs. In the case of serious juvenile offenders, however, the juvenile justice system has appeared impotent to address the appropriate treatment needs of the offenders or the punishment/protection needs of society.

Interestingly, the President's Commission (1967:80) noted that "the great hopes originally held for the juvenile court have not been fulfilled. It has not succeeded significantly in rehabilitating delinquent youth, in reducing or even stemming the tide of delinquency, or in bringing justice and compassion to the child offender." Therefore, we must ask whether these values are important in processing juvenile offenders, even the serious and persistent ones. If these values have relevance, can we expect the adult criminal courts to succeed where the juvenile courts have failed? If they cannot succeed, why should we saddle them with offenders who are not really children, yet in most ways are far from being adults.

The solution seems to be that we must not rely on the criminal justice system to provide the answer; but we should consider modifying the existing juvenile justice system to provide the types of treatment *and* punishment appropriate for the oldest, the most serious, and the most persistent juvenile offenders. This small group obviously needs our focused attention and resources.

Bibliography

Acker, James R. 1987. "Social Sciences and Criminal Law: Capital Punishment by the Numbers—An Analysis of *McClesky v. Kemp.*" *Criminal Law Bulletin,* 23:454–82.

Ageton, Suzanne S. 1983. *Sexual Assault Among Adolescents.* Lexington, MA: Lexington Books.

Agopian, Michael W. 1989. "Targeting Juvenile Gang Offenders for Community Service." *Community Alternatives: International Journal of Family Care* 1:99–108.

Albanese, Jay S. 1985. *Dealing With Delinquency: An Investigation of Juvenile Justice.* Landham, MD: University Press of America.

Alessi, Norman E. et al. 1984. "Suicidal Behavior Among Serious Juvenile Offenders." *American Journal of Psychiatry* 141:286–97.

Alpert, Geoffrey, Ben M. Crouch, and C. Ronald Huff. 1984. "Prison Reform by Judicial Decree: The Unintended Consequences of *Ruiz v. Estelle.*" *Justice System Journal* 9:291–305.

Alschuler, Albert W. 1979. "Plea Bargaining and Its History." *Law and Society Review* 13:211–45.

American Bar Association. 1986. *Criminal and Juvenile Justice Policies: A Roadmap for State Legislators and Policymakers.* Washington, DC: American Bar Association.

American Correctional Association. 1985. "Facility Design: Turning the Page on a New Generation." *Corrections Today* 48:4–87.

American Institutes for Research. 1988. *Evaluation of the Habitual Serious and Violent Juvenile Offender Program.* Washington, DC: Office of Juvenile Justice and Delinquency Prevention.

Anderson, Dennis B., and Donald F. Schoen. 1985. "Diversion Programs: Effect of Stigmatization on Juvenile Status Offenders." *Juvenile and Family Court Journal* 36:13–25.

Armstrong, Troy L., and David M. Altschuler. 1982. "Conflicting Trends in Juvenile Sanctioning: Divergent Strategies in the Handling of the Serious Juvenile Offender." *Juvenile and Family Court Journal* 33:15–30.

Arthur, Lindsay G., 1983. "Dispositions." *Juvenile and Family Court Journal* 34:1–100.

Ashford, Jose B., and Craig Winston LeCroy. 1988. "Decision–making for Juvenile Offenders in Aftercare." *Juvenile and Family Court Journal* 39:47–53.

August, Robin. 1981. *A Study of Juveniles Transferred for Prosecution to the Adult System*. Miami: Office of the Dade-Miami Criminal Justice Council.

————. 1984. *A Study of Juveniles Transferred for Prosecution in the Adult System*. Miami: Office of the Dade-Miami Criminal Justice Council.

Austin, James, and Barry Krisberg. 1981. "Wider, Stronger, and Different Nets: The Dialectics of Criminal Justice Reform." *Journal of Research in Crime and Delinquency* 18:165–96.

————. 1982. "The Unmet Promise of Alternatives to Incarceration." *Crime and Delinquency* 28:374–409.

Bailey, William C. 1983. "Disaggregation in Deterrence and Death Penalty Research: The Case of Murder in Chicago." *Journal of Criminal Law and Criminology* 74:827–59.

————. 1984. "Murder and Capital Punishment in the Nation's Capital." *Justice Quarterly* 1:211–33.

Barnes, Carole Wolfe, and Randal S. Franz. 1989. "Questionably Adult: Determinants and Effects of the Juvenile Waiver Decision." *Justice Quarterly* 6:117–35.

Barney, E. 1986. *Sentencing Young People: What Went Wrong with the Criminal Justice Act 1982?* Brookfield, VT: Gower.

Bartollas, Clemens. 1990. *Juvenile Delinquency* 2d ed. New York: Macmillan.

Bedau, Hugo A. 1982. *The Death Penalty in America*. New York: Oxford University Press.

Benda, Brent B. 1987. "Comparison of Rates of Recidivism among Status Offenders and Delinquents." *Adolescence* 22:445–58.

Bernard, Thomas J. 1987. "Structure and Control: Reconsidering Hirschi's Concept of Commitment." *Justice Quarterly* 4:409–24.

Bienen, Leigh B. et al. 1988. "The Reimposition of Capital Punishment in New Jersey: The Role of Prosecutorial Discretion." *Rutgers Law Review* 41:327–72.

Binder, Arnold. 1979. "The Juvenile Justice System: Where Pretense and Reality Clash." *American Behavioral Scientist* 22:621–52.

———. 1989. "Juvenile Diversion." In *Juvenile Justice: Policies, Programs, and Services*, ed. Albert R. Roberts. Chicago: The Dorsey Press.

Binder, Arnold, and Virginia L. Binder. 1982. "Juvenile Diversion and the Constitution." *Journal of Criminal Justice* 10(1):1–24.

Binder, Arnold, and Gilbert Geis. 1984. "Ad Populum Argumentation in Criminology: Juvenile Diversion as Rhetoric." *Crime and Delinquency* 30:309–33.

Bishop, Donna M., Charles E. Frazier, and John C. Henretta. 1989. "Prosecutorial Waiver: Case Study of a Questionable Reform." *Crime and Delinquency* 35:179–201.

Black, Henry Campbell. 1979. Black's Law Dictionary. St. Paul, MN: West.

Blackmore, John, Marci Brown, and Barry Krisberg. 1988. *Juvenile Justice Reform: The Bellwether States*. Ann Arbor: University of Michigan.

Bortner, M. A. 1988. *Delinquency and Justice: An Age of Crisis*. New York: McGraw-Hill.

———. 1986. "Traditional Rhetoric, Organizational Realities: Remand of Juveniles to Adult Court." *Crime and Delinquency* 32:53–73.

Braithwaite, Lloyd, and Allen Shore. 1981. "Treatment Rhetoric Versus Waiver Decisions." *Journal of Criminal Law and Criminology* 72(4):1867–91.

Brennan, William J. 1986. "The 1986 Oliver Wendell Holmes, Jr. Lecture: Constitutional Adjudication and The Death Penalty: A View from the Court." *Harvard Law Review* 100:313–31.

Brodie, David P. 1986. "The Imposition of the Death Penalty on Juvenile Offenders: How Should Society Respond?" *Journal of Juvenile Law* 10:117–24.

Brown, Waln K., Timothy P. Miller, and Richard L. Jenkins. 1987. "The Favorable Effect of Juvenile Court Adjudication of Delinquent Youth on the First Contact with the Juvenile Justice System." *Juvenile and Family Court Journal* 38:21–26.

Burchard, John D., and Sara Burchard, eds. 1987. *Prevention of Delinquent Behavior*. Newbury Park, CA: Sage.

Bureau of Justice Statistics 1986. *Children in Custody: Public Juvenile Facilities, 1985*. Washington, DC: U.S. Department of Justice.

———. 1988. *BJS Data Report 1987*. Washington, DC: U.S. Department of Justice.

———. 1989. *Children in Custody, 1975–85*. Washington, DC: U.S. Department of Justice.

Burris, Scott. 1987. "Death and a Rational Justice: A Conversation on the Capital Jurisprudence of Justice John Paul Stevens." *Yale Law Journal* 96:521–46.

Cahalan, Margaret W. 1986. *Historical Corrections Statistics in the United States, 1850–1984*. Washington, DC: U.S. Department of Justice.

Calhoun, Thomas, and Brian Pickerill. 1988. "Young Male Prostitutes: Their Knowledge of Selected Sexually Transmitted Diseases." *Psychology* 25:1–8.

Cambridge Survey Research. 1986. *An Analysis of Political Attitudes Towards the Death Penalty in the State of Florida*. Cambridge, MA: Cambridge Survey Research.

Carlson, Nancy D. 1987. "Jailing Juveniles: Impact on Constitutional Rights." *New England Journal on Criminal and Civil Confinement*, 13:45–67.

Carter, Sue. 1984. "Chapter 39, the Florida Juvenile Justice Act: From Juvenile to Adult with the Stroke of a Pen." *Florida State University Law Review* 11:922–47.

"Certification—Burden of Proof: Alaska." 1987. *Juvenile and Family Law Digest* 19(2):97–99.

Challeen, Denis A. 1986. *Making It Right: A Common Sense Approach to Criminal Justice*. Aberdeen, SD: Melius and Peterson.

Chambers, Ola R. 1983. *The Juvenile Offender: A Parole Profile*. Albany, NY: Evaluation and Planning Unit, New York State Division of Parole.

Champion, Dean J. 1987a. "Felony Offenders, Plea Bargaining, and Probation." *Justice Professional* 2:1–18.

———. 1987b. "Guilty Plea Hearings and Judicial Supervision: Some Differences between Federal and State Judges Regarding Rule 11 and a Defendant's Right to Due Process." *American Journal of Criminal Justice* 11:62–81.

———. 1987c. "Probation Trends in Felony Cases: A Look at Prosecutorial Decision-making in Plea Bargaining Agreements." *Journal of Contemporary Criminal Justice* 3:25–37.

———. 1988. *Felony Probation: Problems and Prospects*. New York: Praeger.

———. 1989a. "Teenage Felons and Waiver Hearings: Some Recent Trends, 1980–1988." *Crime and Delinquency* 35:577–85.

———. 1989b. *The U.S. Sentencing Guidelines: Implications for Criminal Justice*. New York: Praeger.

———. 1990. "Juvenile Transfer Trends in Several Southern States." Paper presented at the annual meeting of the Western Society of Criminology, February, Las Vegas.

Cheatwood, Derral. 1988. "The Life-Without-Parole Sanction: Its Current Status and a Research Agenda." *Crime and Delinquency* 34:43–59.

Chicago Police Department, Gang Crimes Section. 1988. *Collecting, Organizing, and Reporting Street Gang Crime*. Chicago: Chicago Police Department.

Clayton, Obie. 1983. "Reconsideration of the Effects of Race in Criminal Sentencing." *Criminal Justice Review* 89:15–20.

Coates, Robert B., Alden D. Miller, and Lloyd E. Ohlin. 1978. *Diversity in a Youth Correctional System: Handling Delinquents in Massachusetts.* Cambridge, MA: Ballinger.

Coffey, Alan R. 1975. *Juvenile Corrections: Treatment and Rehabilitation.* Englewood Cliffs, NJ: Prentice-Hall.

Colley, Lori L., and Robert G. Culbertson. 1988. "Status Offender Legislation and the Courts." *Journal of Offender Counseling, Services, and Rehabilitation* 12:41–56.

Conrad, John P. 1983. "Is There No Alternative to the Hard Line in Juvenile Justice?" *Judicature* 67:162–63.

Conti, Samuel D. et al. 1984. *An Assessment of the Juvenile Justice System in Philadelphia.* Williamsburg, VA: National Center for State Courts.

Cornell, Dewey G. et al. 1987. "Characteristics of Adolescents Charged with Homicide: Review of 72 Cases." *Behavioral Sciences and the Law* 5:11–23.

Cornell, Dewey G., Elissa P. Benedek, and David M. Benedek. 1987. "Juvenile Homicide: Prior Adjustment and a Proposed Typology." *American Journal of Orthopsychiatry* 57:383–93.

Cornish, Tom L. 1982. "Where Have All the Children Gone? Reverse Certification." *Oklahoma Law Review* 35:373–402.

Court Decisions. 1985. "Juveniles—Transfer to Criminal Court—Standard of Review." *Criminal Law Reporter* 38(12):2235.

Cox, Steven M. and John P. Conrad. 1987. *Juvenile Justice: A Guide to Practice and Theory,* 2d ed. Dubuque, IA: Brown.

Cullen, Francis T., and Karen T. Gilbert. 1982. *Reaffirming Rehabilitation.* Cincinnati: Anderson.

Cullen, Francis T., Kathryn M. Golden, and John B. Cullen. 1983. "Is Child Saving Dead? Attitudes Toward Rehabilitation in Illinois." *Journal of Criminal Justice* 11(1):1–13.

Cunniff, Mark A. 1987. *Sentencing Outcomes in 28 Felony Courts, 1985.* Washington, DC: National Association of Criminal Justice Planners.

Curran, Daniel J. 1988. "Destructuring, Privatization, and the Promise of Juvenile Diversion: Compromising Community-based Corrections." *Crime and Delinquency* 34:363–78.

Dahlin, Donald C. 1986. *Models of Court Management.* Milkwood, NY: Associated Faculty Press.

Dale, Michael J. 1987. "The Burger Court and Children's Rights—A Trend Toward Retribution?" *Children's Legal Rights Journal* 8:7–12.

Dannefer, Dale. 1984. "Who Signs the Complaint? Relational Distance and the Juvenile Court Process." *Law and Society Review* 18:249–71.

Datesman, Susan K., and Mikel Aickin. 1985. "Offense Specialization and Escalation among Status Offenders." *Journal of Criminal Law and Criminology* 75:1246–75.

Davis, Samuel M. 1980. *Rights of Juveniles.* New York: Clark Boardman.

Decker, Scott H., ed. 1984. *Juvenile Justice Policy: Analyzing Trends and Outcomes.* Beverly Hills, CA: Sage.

———. 1985. "A Systematic Analysis of Diversion: New Widening and Beyond." *Journal of Criminal Justice* 13:207–16.

Decker, Scott H., and Carol W. Kohfeld. 1984. "A Deterrence Study of the Death Penalty in Illinois, 1933–1980." *Journal of Criminal Justice* 12:367–77.

———. 1986. "The Deterrent Effect of Capital Punishment in Florida: A Time Series Analysis." *Criminal Justice Policy Review* 1:422–37.

———. 1987. "An Empirical Analysis of the Effect of the Death Penalty in Missouri." *Journal of Crime and Justice* 10:23–46.

———. 1988. "Capital Punishment and Executions in the Lone Star State: A Deterrence Study." *Criminal Justice Research Bulletin* 3:1–6.

Dobbert, Duane L. 1987. "Positive Contingency Probation Management." *Juvenile and Family Court Journal* 38:29–33.

Doerner, William G. 1988. "The Impact of Medical Resources on Criminally Induced Lethality: A Further Examination." *Criminology* 26:171–79.

Draper, Thomas, ed. 1985. *Capital Punishment.* New York: H. W. Wilson.

Drowns, Robert W., and Karen M. Hess. 1990. *Juvenile Justice.* St. Paul, MN: West Publishing.

Dunn, Allyson. 1986. "Juvenile Court Records: Confidentiality vs. the Public's Right to Know." *American Criminal Law Review* 23:379–98.

Dwyer, Diane C., and Roger B. McNally. 1987. "Juvenile Justice: Reform, Retain, and Reaffirm." *Federal Probation* 51:47–51.

Ekland-Olson, Sheldon. 1988. "Structured Discretion, Racial Bias, and the Death Penalty: The First Decade After Furman in Texas." *Social Science Quarterly* 69:853–73.

Ellison, W. James. 1987. "State Execution of Juveniles: Defining "Youth" as a Mitigating Factor for Imposing a Sentence Less Than Death." *Law and Psychology Review* 11:1–38.

Fagan, Jeffrey A. 1988. *The Social Organization of Drug Use and Drug Dealing Among Urban Gangs.* New York: John Jay College.

Fagan, Jeffrey A. Martin Forst, and T. Scott Vivona. 1984. "System Processing of Violent Juvenile Offenders: An Empirical Assessment." In *Violent Juvenile Offenders: An Anthology,* ed. Robert A. Mathias, Paul DeMuro, and Richard S. Allison. San Francisco: National Council on Crime and Delinquency.

———. 1987. "Racial Determinants of the Judicial Transfer Decision: Prosecuting Violent Youth in Criminal Court." *Crime and Delinquency* 33:259–86.

Fairchild, Erika C. 1984. "The Scope and Study of Prison Litigation Issues." *Justice System Journal* 9:325–41.

Farnworth, Margaret, Charles E. Frazier, and Anita R. Neuberger. 1988. "Orientations to Juvenile Justice: Exploratory Notes from a Statewide Survey of Juvenile Justice Decisionmakers." *Journal of Criminal Justice* 16:477–91.

Fattah, Ezzat A. 1985. "The Preventive Mechanisms of the Death Penalty: A Discussion." *Crimecare Journal* 1:109–37.

Feld, Barry C. 1981. "Legislative Policies Toward the Serious Juvenile Offender." *Crime and Delinquency* 27(4):497–521.

———. 1984a. "Criminalizing Juvenile Justice: Rules of Procedure for the Juvenile Court." *Minnesota Law Review* 69:141–276.

———. 1984b. "The Decision to Seek Criminal Charges: Just Deserts and the Waiver Decision." *Criminal Justice Ethics* 3(2):27–41.

———. 1987a. "The Juvenile Court Meets the Principle of Offense: Changing Juvenile Justice Sentencing Practices." Unpublished paper presented at the American Society of Criminology meetings, November, Montreal, CAN.

———. 1987b. "The Juvenile Court Meets the Principle of the Offense: Legislative Changes in Juvenile Waiver Statutes." *Journal of Criminal Law and Criminology* 78:471–533.

———. 1988 "The Juvenile Court Meets the Meets the Principle of Offense: Punishment, Treatment, and the Difference it Makes." *Boston University Law Review* 68:821–915.

———. 1989. "The Right to Counsel in Juvenile Court: An Empirical Study of When Lawyers Appear and the Difference It Makes." *Journal of Criminal Law and Criminology* 79:1185–1346.

Finckenauer, James O. 1984. *Juvenile Delinquency and Corrections.* Orlando, FL.: Academic Press.

Fine, Kerry Kinney. 1984. *Alternative Dispute Resolution Programs for Juveniles.* St.Paul, MN: Minnesota House Research Department.

Fisher, R. B. 1984. "Predicting Adolescent Violence." In *The Aggressive Adolescent: Clinical Perspectives,* ed. C. R. Keith. New York: Free Press.

Flanagan, Timothy J., and Edmund F. McGarrell. 1986. *Attitudes of New York Legislators Toward Crime and Criminal Justice: A Report of the State Legislature Survey—1985.* Albany: Hindelang Criminal Justice Research Center, State University of New York at Albany.

Forst, Brian E. 1983. "Capital Punishment and Deterrence: Conflicting Evidence?" *Journal of Criminal Law and Criminology,* 74:927–42.

Forst, Martin, Jeffrey Fagan, and T. Scott Vivona. 1989. "Youth in Prisons and

Training Schools: Perceptions and Consequences of the Treatment-Custody Dichotomy." *Juvenile and Family Court Journal* 40:1–14.

Fox, James G., and Kenneth Viegas. 1987. "The Policy Implications and Impacts of Managing Scarce Juvenile Justice Resources." Unpublished paper presented at the American Society of Criminology meetings, November, Montreal, CAN.

Fraser, Mark, and Michael Norman. 1988. "Chronic Juvenile Delinquency and the 'Suppression Effect': An Exploratory Study." *Journal of Offender Counseling, Services, and Rehabilitation* 13:55–73.

Frazier, Charles E. 1989. "Preadjudicatory Detention." In *Juvenile Justice: Policies, Programs, and Services*, ed. Albert R. Roberts. Chicago: The Dorsey Press.

Friedlander, Robert A. 1987. "Socrates Was Right: Propositions in Support of Capital Punishment." *New England Journal on Criminal and Civil Confinement* 13:1–9.

Galbo, Andrea. 1985. "Death after Life: The Future of New York's Mandatory Death Penalty for Murders Committed by Life-term Prisoners." *Fordham Urban Law Journal* 13:597–638.

Garbarino, James, Janis Wilson, and A. C. Garbarino. 1986. "The Adolescent Runaway." In *Troubled Youths, Troubled Families*, eds. James Garbarino et al. Hawthrone, NY: Aldine.

Gelber, Seymour. 1988. *Hard-core Delinquents: Reaching Out Through the Miami Experiment*. Birmingham: University of Alabama Press.

Geller, Mark, and Lynn Ford-Somma. 1984. *Violent Homes, Violent Children*. Trenton, NJ: Division of Juvenile Services, New Jersey Department of Corrections.

Georgia Commission on Juvenile Justice. 1985. *Strengthening Juvenile Justice in Georgia*. Atlanta: Georgia Commission on Juvenile Justice.

Gillespie, L. Kay and Michael D. Norman. 1984. "Does Certification Mean Prison: Some Preliminary Findings from Utah." *Juvenile and Family Court Journal* 35:23–34.

Glick, Henry R. 1983. *Courts, Politics, and Justice*. New York: McGraw-Hill.

Goldstein, Arnold P. and Barry Glick. 1987. *Aggression Replacement Training: A Comprehensive Intervention for Aggressive Youths*. Champaign, IL: Research Press.

Goodstein, Lynne, and John Hepburn. 1985. *Determinate Sentencing and Imprisonment: A Failure of Reform*. Cincinnati, OH: Anderson.

Goodstein, Lynne, and Henry Southeimer. 1987. "Evaluating Correctional Placements Through the Use of Failure Rate Analysis." Paper presented at the American Society of Criminology meetings, November, Montreal, CAN.

Greenwood, Peter W. 1986. "Differences in Criminal Behavior and Court Responses among Juvenile and Adult Defendants." In *An Annual Review of Research*, eds. Michael Tonry and Norval Morris. vol. 7. Chicago: University of Chicago Press.

Griffiths, Curt Taylor. 1988. "Community-based Corrections for Young Offenders: Proposal for a 'Localized' Corrections." *International Journal of Comparative and Applied Criminal Justice* 12:219–28.

Grisso, Thomas. 1981. *Juveniles' Waiver of Rights: Legal and Psychological Competence*. New York: Plenum.

Grisso, Thomas, Alan Tomkins, and Pamela Casey. 1988. "Psychosocial Concepts in Juvenile Law." *Law and Human Behavior* 12:403–38.

Gross, Samuel R., and Robert Mauro. 1984. "Patterns of Death: An Analysis of Racial Disparities in Capital Sentencing and Homicide Victimization." *Stanford Law Review* 37:27–153.

———. 1989. *Death and Discrimination: Racial Disparities in Capital Sentencing*. Boston: Northeastern University Press.

Hackler, James C. 1978. "The Need to Do Something," In *The Prevention of Youthful Crime: The Great Stumble Forward*. Toronto: Methuen Press.

Hagedorn, John. 1988. *People and Folks: Gangs, Crime, and the Underclass in a Rusbelt City*. Chicago, IL: Lake View Press.

Hahn, Paul A. 1978. *The Juvenile Offender and the Law*, 2d ed. Cincinnati: Anderson.

Haizlip, T., B. F. Corder, and B. C. Ball. 1984. "The Adolescent Murderer." In *The Aggressive Adolescent: Clinical Perspectives*, ed. C. R. Keith. New York: Free Press.

Hamparian, Donna M. et al. 1982. *Youth in Adult Courts: Between Two Worlds*. Columbus, OH: Academy for Contemporary Problems.

Hancock, Paula, and Katherine Teilmann Van Dusen. 1985. *Attorney Representation in Juvenile Court: A Comparison of Public Defenders and Privately Retained Counsel*. Washington, DC: U.S. Office of Juvenile Justice and Delinquency Prevention.

Hans, Valeria P. and Neil Vidmar. 1986. *Judging the Jury*. New York: Plenum.

Hanson, Kweku. 1988 "Racial Disparities and the Law of Death: The Case for a New Hard Look at Race-Based Challenges to Capital Punishment." *National Black Law Journal* 10:298–317.

Harris, Patricia M. 1988. "Juvenile Sentence Reform and Its Evaluation: A Demonstration of the Need for More Precise Measures of Offense Seriousness in Juvenile Justice Research." *Evaluation Review* 12:655–66.

Harris, Patricia M., and Lisa Graff. 1988. "A Critique of Juvenile Sentence Reform." *Federal Probation* 52:66–71.

Hartstone, Eliot, and Karen V. Hansen. 1984. "The Violent Juvenile Offender:

An Empirical Portrait." In *Violent Juvenile Offenders: An Anthology*. Robert A. Mathias, Paul DeMuro, and Richard S. Allison. San Francisco: National Council on Crime and Delinquency.

Hartstone, Eliot, Ellen Slaughter, and Jeffrey Fagan. 1986. *The Colorado Juvenile Justice System Processing of Violent, Serious, and Minority Youths*. San Francisco: URSA Institute.

Harvard Law Review. 1986. "The Cultural Defense in the Criminal Law." *Harvard Law Review*, 99:1293–1311.

Hasenfeld, Yeheskel, and Paul P. L. Cheung. 1985. "The Juvenile Court as a People-Processing Organization: A Political Economy Perspective." *American Journal of Sociology* 90:801–24.

Hastie, Reid, Steven D. Penrod, and Nancy Pennington. 1983. *Inside the Jury*. Cambridge: Harvard University Press.

Hawaii Crime Commission. 1985. *The Serious Juvenile Offender in Hawaii*. Honolulu: Hawaii Crime Commission.

Hawaii Criminal Justice Commission. 1986. *The Waiver of Juveniles in Hawaii*. Honolulu: Hawaii Criminal Justice Commission.

Hawkins, J. David, and Tony Lamb. 1987. "Teacher Practices, Social Development, and Delinquency." In *Prevention of Delinquent Behavior*, eds. John D. Burchard and Sara Burchard. Newbury Park, CA: Sage.

Heilbrun, Alfred B. Jr., Allison Foster, and Jill Golden. 1989. "The Death Sentence in Georgia, 1974–1987: Criminal Justice or Racial Injustice?" *Criminal Justice and Behavior* 16:139–54.

Hengstler, Gary. 1987. "Attorneys for the Damned." *American Bar Association Journal* 73:56–60.

Heuser, James Paul. 1985. *Juveniles Arrested for Serious Felony Crimes in Oregon and "Remanded" to Adult Criminal Courts: A Statistical Study*. Salem, OR: Oregon Department of Justice, Crime Analysis Center.

Hingson, Ralph, Timothy Heeren, and Suzette Morelock. 1989. "Effects of Maine's 1982.02 Law to Reduce Teenage Driving After Drinking." *Alcohol, Drugs, and Driving*, 5:25–36.

Hochstedler, Ellen. 1986. "Criminal Prosecution of the Mentally Disordered." *Law and Society Review* 20:279–92.

Huff, C. Ronald, and Geoffrey P. Alpert. 1982. "Organizational Compliance with Court-Ordered Prison Reform." In *Implementing Criminal Justice Policies*, ed. Merry Morash. Beverly Hills: Sage.

Humphrey, John A., and Timothy J. Fogarty. 1987. "Race and Plea Bargained Outcomes: A Research Note." *Social Forces* 66:176–82.

Innes, Christopher A. 1988. *Profile of State Prison Inmates, 1987*. Washington, DC: U.S. Department of Justice.

Iovanni, Lee Ann. 1987. "Racial Disparity in Capital Sentencing in North

Carolina." Paper presented at the American Society of Criminology meetings, November. Montreal, CAN.

Ito, Jeanne A. 1984. *Measuring the Performance for Different Types of Juvenile Courts*. Williamsburg, VA: National Center for State Courts.

Jacobs, Nancy F., Ellen Chayet, and Charles Meara. 1986. *Bang the Gavel Slowly: Felony Case Processing in New York City's Supreme Court*. New York: Criminal Justice Center, John Jay College of Criminal Justice.

Jamieson, Katherine M., and Timothy J. Flanagan. 1989. *Sourcebook of Criminal Justice Statistics—1988*. Washington, DC: U.S. Government Printing Office.

Just, Rona L. 1985. "Executing Youthful Offenders: The Unanswered Question in *Eddings v. Oklahoma*." *Fordham Urban Law Journal* 13:471–510.

Karraker, N., D. E. Macallair, and V. N. Schiraldi. 1988. *Public Safety with Care: A Model System for Juvenile Justice in Hawaii*. Alexandria, VA: National Center on Institutions and Alternatives.

Keith, C. R. ed. 1984. *The Aggressive Adolescent: Clinical Perspectives*. New York: Free Press.

Kempf, K. L., and R. L. Austin. 1986. "Older and More Recent Evidence on Racial Discrimination in Sentencing." *Journal of Quantitative Criminology* 2:29–48.

Kimbrough, Jackie. 1986. "School-based Strategies for Delinquency Prevention." In *Intervention Strategies for Chronic Juvenile Offenders: Some New Perspectives*, ed. Peter W. Greenwood. Westport, CT: Greenwood Press.

Kittel, Norman G. 1987. "Criminal Defense Attorneys: Bottom of the Legal Profession's Class System." *Justice Professional* 2:44–59.

Kratcoski, Peter C. 1985. "Youth Violence Directed Toward Significant Others." *Journal of Adolescence* 8:145–57.

Kriesman, J., and R. Siden. 1982. *Juvenile Homicide: A Literature Review*. Berkeley: University of California-Berkeley, California Office of Criminal Justice Planning.

Krisberg, Barry. 1988. *The Juvenile Court Reclaiming the Vision*. San Francisco: National Council on Crime and Delinquency.

Kueneman, Rod, Rick Linden, and Rick Kosmick. 1985. *A Study of Manitoba's Northern and Rural Juvenile Courts*. Manitoba, CAN: University of Manitoba.

Kufeldt, Kathleen, and Phillip E. Perry. 1989. "Running Around with Runaways." *Community Alternatives: International Journal of Family Care* 1:85–97.

Lab, Steven P. 1984. "Patterns in Juvenile Misbehavior." *Crime and Delinquency* 30:293–308.

LaFree, Gary D. 1985. "Official Reactions to Hispanic Defendants in the Southwest." *Journal of Research on Crime and Delinquency* 22:213–237.

Laub, John H., and Bruce K. MacMurray. 1987. "Increasing the Prosecutor's Role in Juvenile Court: Expectations and Realities." *Justice System Journal* 12:196–209.

Law Enforcement Assistance Administration. 1980. *Juvenile Justice: Before and After the Onset of Delinquency.* Washington, DC: U.S. Department of Justice.

Lawrence, Richard A. 1984. "The Role of Legal Counsel in Juveniles' Understanding of Their Rights." *Juvenile and Family Court Journal* 34:49–58.

Lerman, Paul. 1984 "Child Welfare, the Private Sector, and Community-based Corrections." *Crime and Delinquency* 30:5–38.

Lester, David. 1987. *The Death Penalty: Issues and Answers.* Springfield, IL: Thomas.

Loeber, Ralph, and Thomas J. Dishion. 1987. "Antisocial and Delinquent Youths: Methods for Their Early Identification." In *Prevention of Delinquent Behavior*, eds. John D. Burchard and Sara Burchard. Newbury Park, CA: Sage.

Logan, Charles H., and Sharla P. Rausch. 1985. "Why Deinstitutionalizing Status Offenders is Pointless." *Crime and Delinquency* 31:501–517.

Lombardo, Rita, and Janet DiGiorgio-Miller. 1988. "Concepts and Techniques in Working with Juvenile Sex Offenders." *Journal of Offender Counseling, Services, and Rehabilitation* 13:39–53.

Lundman, Richard J. 1986. "Beyond Probation: Assessing the Generalizability of the Delinquency Suppression Effect Measures Reported by Murray and Cox." *Crime and Delinquency* 32:134–47.

Mahoney, Anne Rankin. 1985a. "Time and Process in Juvenile Court." *Justice System Journal* 1:37–55.

———. 1985b "Jury Trials for Juveniles: Right or Ritual?" *Justice Quarterly* 2:553–65.

Maloney, Dennis, Dennis Romig, and Troy Armstrong. 1988. "Juvenile Probation: the Balanced Approach." *Juvenile and Family Court Journal* 39:1–63.

Margolis, Richard J. 1988. *Out of Harm's Way: The Emancipation of Juvenile Justice.* New York: Edna McConnell Clark Foundation.

Markman, Stephen J., and Paul G. Cassell. 1988. "Protecting the Innocent: A Response to the Bedau-Radelet Study." *Stanford Law Review* 41:121–70.

Masur, Louis P. 1988. "The Revision of the Criminal Law in Post-Revolutionary America." In *Criminal Justice History: An International Annual, Vol. 8, 1987.* Westport, CT: Meckler.

Mathias, Robert A., Paul DeMuro, and Richard S. Allinson. 1984 *Violent Juvenile Offenders: An Anthology*. San Francisco: National Council on Crime and Delinquency.

Maxon, Cheryl L., Margaret A. Gordon, and Malcolm W. Klein. 1986. "Differences Between Gang and Nongang Homicides." *Criminology* 23:209–22.

Mays, G. Larry. 1980. "Let's Do Away With the Juvenile Court: A Critical Look at Juvenile Justice." *Journal of Humanics* 8(2):74–89.

———. 1989. "The Impact of Federal Sentencing Guidelines on Jail and Prison Overcrowding and Early Release." In *The U.S. Sentencing Guidelines: Implications for Criminal Justice*, ed. Dean J. Champion. New York: Praeger.

Mays, G. Larry, and William A. Taggart. 1985. "The Impact of Litigation on Changing New Mexico Prison Conditions." *The Prison Journal* 65:38–53.

McCarthy, Belinda R. 1987a. "Case Attrition in the Juvenile Court: An Application of the Crime Control Model." *Justice Quarterly* 4:237–55.

———. 1987b *Intermediate Punishments: Intensive Supervision, Home Confinement, and Electronic Surveillance*. Monsey, NY: Willow Tree Press.

———. 1989. "A Preliminary Research Model for the Juvenile and Family Court." *Juvenile and Family Court Journal* 40:43–48.

McCord, William, and Jose Sanchez. 1983. "The Treatment of Deviant Children: A Twenty-five Year Follow-up Study." *Crime and Delinquency* 29:238–53.

McDermott, M. Joan et al. 1985. *Pins Intake Project; Final Report*. Albany, NY: Office of Policy Analysis, Research and Statistical Services, New York State Division of Criminal Justice Services.

McDermott, M. Joan, and John H. Laub. 1987. "Adolescence and Juvenile Justice Policy." *Criminal Justice Policy Review* 1:438–55.

McDonald, William F. 1985. *Plea Bargaining: Critical Issues and Common Practices*. Washington, DC: U.S. Department of Justice.

McIntyre, Lisa J. 1987. *The Public Defender: The Practice of Law in the Shadows of Repute*. Chicago: University of Chicago Press.

McShane, Marilyn D., and Frank P. Williams III. 1989. "The Prison Adjustment of Juvenile Offenders." *Crime and Delinquency* 35:254–69.

Menard, Scott. 1987. "Short-term Trends in Crime and Delinquency: A Comparison of UCR, NCS, and Self-Report Data." *Justice Quarterly* 4:455–74.

Metchik, Eric. 1987a. "Predicting Pre-Trial Behavior of Juvenile Offenders in Adult Court." Paper presented at the American Society of Criminology meetings, November. Montreal, CAN.

————. 1987b. *Recommending Juvenile Offenders for Pretrial Release*. New York: New York City Criminal Justice Agency.

Michigan Law Review. 1983. "Access to Juvenile Delinquency Hearings." *Michigan Law Review* 81:1540–65.

Miller, Frank W. et al. 1985. *The Juvenile Justice Process*. Mineola, NY: Foundation Press.

Miller, M. O., and M. Gold. 1984. "Iatrogenesis in the Juvenile Justice System." *Youth and Society* 16:83–111.

Miller, Marc. 1986a. "Legal Constraints on Intervention Programs in Public Schools." In *Intervention Strategies for Chronic Juvenile Offenders: Some New Perspectives*, ed. Peter W. Greenwood. Westport, CT: Greenwood Press.

————. 1986b. "Changing Legal Paradigms in Juvenile Justice." In *Intervention Strategies for Chronic Juvenile Offenders: Some New Perspectives*, ed. Peter W. Greenwood. Westport, CT: Greenwood Press.

Mones, Paul. 1984. "Too Many Rights or Not Enough? A Study of the Juvenile Related Decisions of the West Virginia Supreme Court of Appeals." *Journal of Juvenile Law* 8:32–57.

Moore, Richter H. 1976. "The Criminal Justice Non-system." In *Readings in Criminal Justice*, ed. Richter H. Moore, Thomas C. Marks, and Robert V. Barrow. Indianapolis: Bobbs-Merrill.

Nagoshi, Jack T. 1986. *Juvenile Recidivism: Third Circuit Court*. Honolulu: Youth Development and Research Center.

National Advisory Committee for Juvenile Justice and Delinquency Prevention. 1980. *Standards for the Administration of Juvenile Justice*. Washington, DC: U.S. Department of Justice.

National Advisory Committee on Criminal Justice Standards and Goals. 1976. *Juvenile Justice and Delinquency Prevention*. Washington, DC: U.S. Government Printing Office.

National College of Juvenile and Family Law. 1989. "Court-Approved Alternative Dispute Resolution: A Better Way to Resolve Minor Delinquency, Status Offense, and Abuse/Neglect Cases." *Juvenile and Family Court Journal* 40:51–98.

National Council of Juvenile and Family Court Judges. 1984. *The Juvenile Court and Serious Offenders: 38 Recommendations*. Reno, NV: National Council of Juvenile Delinquency and Family Court Judges.

————. 1986. "Deprived Children: A Judicial Response—73 Recommendations." *Juvenile and Family Court Journal* 37:3–48.

Neubauer, David W. 1988. *America's Courts and the Criminal Justice System*, 3d ed. Pacific Grove, CA: Brooks/Cole Publishing Co.

New Jersey Division of Criminal Justice. 1985. *Juvenile Waivers to Adult Court: A Report to the New Jersey State Legislature*. Trenton: New Jersey Division of Criminal Justice.

New Mexico Statutes Annotated. 1978. *New Mexico Statutes Annotated*. Charlotteville, VA: The Michie Co.

New York State Division of Parole. 1985. *PARJO III: Final Evaluation of the PARJO Pilot Supervision Program*. Albany: New York State Division of Parole, Evaluation and Planning Unit.

Nimick, Ellen, Linda Szymanski, and Howard Snyder. 1986. *Juvenile Court Waiver: A Study of Juvenile Court Cases Transferred to Criminal Court*. Pittsburgh: National Center for Juvenile Justice.

Norman, Michael D. 1986. "Discretionary Justice: Decision Making in a State Juvenile Parole Board." *Juvenile and Family Court Journal* 37:19–25.

Note 1982. "The Expanding Scope of Prosecutorial Discretion in Charging Juveniles as Adults: A Critical Look at *People v. Thorpe*." *University of Colorado Law Review*, 54(1):617–35.

Office of Juvenile Justice and Delinquency Prevention. 1980a. *Children in Custody: Advance Report on the 1979 Census of Private Juvenile Facilities*. Washington, DC: U.S. Department of Justice.

———. 1980b. *Children in Custody*: Advance Report on the 1979 Census of Public Juvenile Facilities. Washington, DC: U.S. Department of Justice.

———. 1987. *Juvenile Court Statistics 1984*. Washington, DC: U.S. Department of Justice.

———. 1989. *Juvenile Court Statistics 1985*. Washington, DC: U.S. Department of Justice.

Ogletree, Charles J. 1987. "Are Confessions Really Good for the Soul?: A Proposal to Mirandize *Miranda*." *Harvard Law Review* 100:1826–45.

Ohio Revised Code. 1987. *Ohio Revised Code*. Columbus, OH: Ohio Revised Code.

Orlando, Frank A., Allen F. Breed, and Robert L. Smith. 1987. *Juvenile Justice Reform: A Critique of the A.L.E.C. Code*. Minneapolis: Hubert Humphrey Institute of Public Affairs, University of Minnesota.

Osbun, Lee Ann, and Peter A. Rode. 1984. "Prosecuting Juveniles as Adults: The Quest for 'Objective' Decisions." *Criminology* 22:187–202.

Paternoster, Raymond. 1984. "Prosecutorial Discretion in Requesting the Death Penalty: A Case of Victim-Based Racial Discrimination." *Law and Society Review* 9:357–401.

Petersilia, Joan M. 1983. *Racial Disparities in the Criminal Justice System*. Washington, DC: U.S. Department of Justice, National Institute of Corrections.

———. 1985. *Probation and Felony Offenders*. Washington, DC: U.S. Department of Justice, Bureau of Justice Statistics.

Peterson, Ruth D., and William C. Bailey. 1988. "Murder and Capital Punishment in the Evolving Context of the Post-Furman Era." *Social Forces* 66:774–807.

Pindur, W., and D. K. Wells. 1985. "New Directions for Juvenile Justice."
    Police Chief 52:24–26.
Pingree, David. H. 1984. "Florida Youth Services." *Corrections Today* 46:60–
    61.
Platt, Anthony M. 1977. *The Child Savers: The Invention of Delinquency*, 2d
    ed. Chicago: University of Chicago Press.
Plutichik, Robert. 1983. "Variables Correlated with Violent Behavior in Young
    Children." *International Journal of Offender Therapy and Compar-
    ative Criminology* 27:66–70.
Polen, Charles A. 1987. "Youth on Death Row: Waiver of Juvenile Court
    Jurisdiction and Imposition of the Death Penalty on Juvenile Of-
    fenders." *Northern Kentucky Law Review* 13:495–517.
Polk, Kenneth. 1987. "When Less Means More: An Analysis of Destructuring
    in Criminal Justice." *Crime and Delinquency* 33:358–78.
Pratt, John, and Roger Grimshaw. 1983. "A Juvenile Justice Pre-Court Tribunal
    At Work." *Howard Journal of Criminal Justice* 24:213–28.
President's Commission on Law Enforcement and the Administration of Jus-
    tice. 1967. *The Challenge of Crime in a Free Society*. Washington, DC:
    U.S. Government Printing Office.
Price, Larry R. 1990. "Juvenile Justice: Designed to Help." *Perspectives* 14:6–
    7.
Radelet, Michael R., ed. 1989. *Facing the Death Penalty: Essays on Cruel and
    Unusual Punishment*. Philadelphia: Temple University Press.
Radelet, Michael R., and Margaret Vandiver. 1983. "The Florida Supreme
    Court and Death Penalty Appeals." *Journal of Criminal Law and
    Criminology* 74:913–26.
Rankin, J. H., and L. E. Wells. 1985. "From Status to Delinquent Offenses:
    Escalation?" *Journal of Criminal Justice* 13:171–80.
Reed, David. 1983. *Needed: Serious Solutions for Serious Juvenile Crime*.
    Chicago: Chicago Law Enforcement Study.
Regnery, Alfred S. 1989. "Getting Away With Murder: Why the Juvenile Justice
    System Needs an Overhaul." In *Taking Sides: Clashing Views on
    Controversial Issues in Crime and Criminology*, ed. Richard C. Monk.
    Guilford, CT: Dushkin Publishing Group.
Reichel, Philip, and Carole Seyfrit. 1984. "A Peer Jury in the Juvenile Court."
    Crime and Delinquency 30:423–38.
Reuterman, Nicholas A., and Thomas R. Hughes. 1984. "Developments in
    Juvenile Justice During the Decade of the 70s: Juvenile Detention
    Facilities." *Journal of Criminal Justice* 12:325–33.
Ricotta, Dominic J. 1988. "Eighth Amendment—the Death Penalty for Juve-
    niles: A State's Right or a Child's Injustice?" *Journal of Criminal Law
    and Criminology* 79:821–52.

Roberts, Albert R. 1989. *Juvenile Justice: Politics, Programs, and Services.* Chicago: The Dorsey Press.

Robertson, John A., ed. 1974. *Rough Justice: Perspectives on Lower Criminal Courts.* Boston: Little, Brown and Company.

Rogers, Joseph W., and G. Larry Mays. 1987. *Juvenile Delinquency and Juvenile Justice.* New York: Wiley.

Rogers, Richard, and Robert M. Wettstein eds. 1987. "Death Penalty." *Behavioral Sciences and the Law* 5:381–494.

Rojek, Dean, and Maynard L. Erickson. 1982. "Delinquent Careers: A Test of the Career Escalation Model." *Criminology* 20(1):5–28.

Rosner, Lydia S. 1988. "Juvenile Secure Detention." *Journal of Offender Counseling, Services, and Rehabilitation* 12:77–93.

Rossum, Ralph A., Benedict J. Koller, and C. Manfredi. 1987. *Juvenile Justice Reform: A Model for the States.* Claremont, CA: Rose Institute of State and Local Government and the American Legislative Council.

Rubin, H. Ted. 1980. "The Emerging Prosecutor Dominance of the Juvenile Court Intake Process." *Crime and Delinquency* 26(3):299–318.

———. 1984. *The Courts: Fulcrum of the Justice System*, 2d ed. New York: Random House.

———. 1985a. *Behind the Black Robes: Juvenile Court Judges and the Court.* Beverly Hills: Sage.

———. 1985b. *Juvenile Justice: Policy, Practice, and Law.* 2d ed. New York: Random House.

———. 1988. "Fulfilling Juvenile Restitution Requirements in Community Correctional Programs." *Federal Probation* 52:32–42.

———. 1989. "The Juvenile Court Landscape." In *Juvenile Justice: Policies, Programs, and Services*, ed. Albert R. Roberts. Chicago: The Dorsey Press.

Rudman, Cary et al. 1986. "Violent Youth in Adult Court: Process and Punishment." *Crime and Delinquency* 32:75–96.

Rutherford, Andrew. 1986. *Growing Out of Crime.* New York: Penguin.

Rydell, Peter C. 1986. "The Economics of Early Intervention versus Later Incarceration." In *Intervention Strategies for Chronic Juvenile Offenders: Some New Perspectives*, ed. Peter M. Greenwood. Westport, CT: Greenwood Press.

Sagatun, Inger, and Leonard P. Edwards. 1988. "The Disposition of Juvenile Records: An Interagency Comparison." *Juvenile and Family Court Journal* 39:37–45.

Sagatun, Inger, Loretta L. McCollum, and Leonard P. Edwards. 1985. "The Effect of Transfers from Juvenile Court to Criminal Court: A Loglinear Analysis." *Journal of Crime and Justice* 8:65–92.

Sametz, Lynn. 1984. "Revamping the Adolescent's Justice System to Serve the

Needs of the Very Young Offender." *Juvenile and Family Court Journal* 34:21–30.

Schack, Elizabeth T., and Hermine Nessen. 1984. *The Experiment That Failed: The New York Juvenile Offender Law—A Study Report.* New York: Citizen's Committee for Children of New York.

Schlossman, Steven L. 1977. *Love and the American Delinquent.* Chicago: University of Chicago Press.

Schneider, Anne Larson. 1984a. "Divesting Status Offenses from Juvenile Court Jurisdiction." *Crime and Delinquency* 30:347–70.

———. 1984b. "Sentencing Guidelines and Recidivism Rates of Juvenile Offenders." *Justice Quarterly* 1(1):107–24.

———. 1985. *Reports of the National Juvenile Justice Assessment Centers: The Impact of Deinstitutionalization on Recidivism and Secure Confinement of Status Offenders.* Washington, DC: U.S. Department of Justice.

Schneider, Anne Larson, and Donna D. Schram. 1986. "The Washington State Juvenile Justice System Reform: A Review of Findings." *Criminal Justice Policy Review* 1:211–35.

Schulhofer, Stephen J. 1986. "The Future of the Adversary System." *Justice Quarterly* 3:83–93.

Schwartz, Ira M. 1989. *(In) Justice for Juveniles: Rethinking the Best of the Child.* Lexington, MA: Lexington Books.

Scoville, James C. 1987. "Deadly Mistakes: Harmless Error in Capital Sentencing." *University of Chicago Law Review* 54:740–58.

Seljan, B. J. 1983. *Juvenile Justice System Professional Survey: A Description of Results in the National Evaluation Sites.* Eugene, OR.: Institute of Policy Analysis.

Seyfrit, Carole L., Phillip L. Reichel, and Brian L. Stutts. 1987. "Peer Juries as a Juvenile Justice Diversion Technique." *Youth and Society* 18:302–16.

Shelden, Randall, and John A. Horvath. 1987. "Intake Processing in a Juvenile Court: A Comparison of Legal and Nonlegal Variables." *Juvenile and Family Court Journal* 38:13–19.

Shelden, Randall G., John A. Horvath, and Sharon Tracy. 1989. "Do Status Offenders Get Worse? Some Clarifications on the Question of Escalation." *Crime and Delinquency* 35:202–16.

Sheleff, Leon Shaskolsky. 1987. *Ultimate Penalties: Capital Punishment, Life Imprisonment, Physical Torture.* Columbus: Ohio State University Press.

Sikorski, John B., and Thomas P. McGee. 1986. "Learning Disabilities and the Juvenile Justice System." *Juvenile and Family Court Journal* 37:1–97.

Simonsen, Clifford E., and Marshall S. Gordon, III. 1982. *Juvenile Justice in America*, 2d ed. New York: Macmillan.

Singer, Simon I. 1985. *Relocating Juvenile Crime: The Shift from Juvenile to Criminal Justice*. Albany: Nelson A. Rockefeller Institute of Government, State University of New York.

Smith, George C. 1986. *Capital Punishment 1986: Last Lines of Defense*. Washington, DC: Washington Legal Foundation.

Smith, M. Dwayne. 1987. "Patterns of Discrimination in Assessments of the Death Penalty: The Case of Louisiana." *Journal of Criminal Justice* 15:279–86.

Smykla, John Ortiz. 1987. "The Human Impact of Capital Punishment: Interviews with Families of Persons on Death Row." *Journal of Criminal Justice* 15:331–47.

Snellenburg, Sidney C. 1986. "A Normative Alternative to the Death Penalty." Paper presented at a meeting of the Southern Association of Criminal Justice Educators, October. Atlanta, GA.

Snyder, Howard N. 1987. "A National Portrait of Juvenile Court Caseloads: A Summary of Delinquency in the United States 1983." *Juvenile and Family Court Journal* 31(1):39–53.

Snyder, Howard N., John Hutzler, and Terrence Finnegan. 1985. *Delinquency in the United States 1982*. Pittsburgh: National Center for Juvenile Justice.

Speck, Nan B., Dean W. Ginther, and Joseph R. Helton. 1988. "Runaways Who Will Run Away Again." *Adolescence* 23:881–8.

Speirs, Verne L. 1988. *A Private-Sector Corrections Program for Juveniles: Paint Creek Youth Center*. Washington, DC: U.S. Department of Justice.

———. 1989. *The Juvenile Court's Response to Violent Crime*. Washington, DC: Office of Justice Programs.

Spergel, Irving A. 1986. "The Violent Gang Problem in Chicago: A Local Community Approach." *Social Service Review* 60:94–131.

Spohn, Cassia, John Gruhl, and Susan Welch. 1987. "The Impact of the Ethnicity and Gender of Defendants on the Decision to Reject or Dismiss Felony Charges." *Criminology* 25:175–91.

Spohn, Cassia, Susan Welch, and John Gruhl. 1985. "Women Defendants in Court: The Interaction Between Sex and Race in Convicting and Sentencing." *Social Science Quarterly* 66:178–85.

Springer, Charles E. 1987. *Justice for Juveniles*. Rockville, MD: National Institute for Juvenile Justice and Delinquency Prevention.

Steen, Charlene, and Barbara Monnette. 1989. *Treating Adolescent Sex Offenders in the Community*. Springfield, IL: Charles Thomas.

Steinhart, David. 1988. *California Opinion Poll: Public Attitudes on Youth Crime*. San Francisco: National Council on Crime and Delinquency.

Stewart, Mary Janet, Edward L. Vockell, and Rose E. Ray. 1986. "Decreasing Court Appearances of Juvenile Status Offenders." *Social Casework* 67:74–79.

Stitt, B. Grant, and Sheldon Siegel. 1986. "The Ethnics of Plea Bargaining." Paper presented at the Academy of Criminal Justice Sciences meetings, April. Orlando, FL.

Strasburg, Paul A. 1984. "Recent National Trends in Serious Juvenile Crime." In *Violent Juvenile Offenders: An Anthology*, eds. Robert A. Mathias, Paul DeMuro, and Richard S. Allison. San Francisco: National Council on Crime and Delinquency.

Streib, Victor L. 1983. "Death Penalty for Children: The American Experience with Capital Punishment for Crimes Committed while under Age Eighteen." *Oklahoma Law Review* 36: 613–41.

———. 1987. *Death Penalty for Juveniles.* Bloomington: Indiana University Press.

Streib, Victor L., and Lynn Sametz. 1988. *Capital Punishment of Female Juveniles.* Paper presented at the 1988 meeting of the American Society of Criminology, November. Chicago.

Sutton, John R. 1985. "The Juvenile Court and Social Welfare: Dynamics of Progressive Reform." *Law and Society Review* 19:107–45.

Szymanski, Linda A. 1989. *Waiver/Transfer/Certification of Juveniles to Criminal Court: Age Restrictions; Crime Restrictions.* Pittsburgh: National Center for Juvenile Justice.

Takata, Susan R., and Richard G. Zevitz. 1987. "Youth Gangs in Racine: An Examination of Community Perceptions." *Wisconsin Sociologist* 24:132–41.

Task Force on Juvenile Delinquency. 1967. *Juvenile Delinquency and Youth Crime.* Washington, DC: U.S. Government Printing Office.

Teschner, Douglass P., and John J. Wolter eds. 1984. *Wilderness Challenge: Outdoor Education Alternatives for Youth in Need.* Hadlyme, CT: Institute of Experimental Studies.

Thomas, Charles W., and Shay Bilchik. 1985. "Prosecuting Juveniles in Criminal Courts: A Legal and Empirical Analysis." *Journal of Criminal Law and Criminology* 76:439–79.

Thomas, Robert H., and John D. Hutcheson. 1986. *Georgia Residents' Attitudes Toward the Death Penalty: The Disposition of Juvenile Offenders and Related Issues.* Atlanta: Center for Public and Urban Research, Georgia State University.

Thomson, Doug, and Patrick D. McAnany. 1984. "Punishment and Responsibility in Juvenile Court: Deserts-based Probation for Delinquents." In *Probation and Parole: Reconsideration of a Mission*, ed. Patrick D. McAnany, Doug Thomson, and David Fogel. Cambridge, MA: Oelgeschlager, Gunn, and Hain.

Thornberry, Terence, and R. L. Christenson. 1984. "Juvenile Justice Decision-making as a Longitudinal Process." *Social Forces* 63:433–44.

Tittle, Charles R., and Debra A. Curran. 1988. "Contingencies for Dispositional Disparities in Juvenile Justice." *Social Forces* 67:23–58.

Tracy, Paul. 1987. "Juvenile Waiver: Problems in Prediction." Paper presented at the American Society of Criminology meetings, November. Montreal, CAN.

"Transfer/Due Process/Equal Protection: Rhode Island" 1979 *Juvenile Law Digest* 11(9): 274–76.

Treanor, William W., and Adrienne E. Volenik. 1987. *The New Right's Juvenile Crime and Justice Agenda for the States: A Legislator's Briefing Book.* Washington, DC: American Youth Work Center.

Trester, Harold B. 1981. *Supervision of the Offender.* Englewood Cliffs, NJ: Prentice-Hall.

U.S. Bureau of Justice Statistics. 1988. *Criminal Justice Information Policy: Juvenile Records and Recordkeeping Systems.* Washington, DC: U.S. Government Printing Office.

U.S. Code. 1990. *United States Code Annotated.* St. Paul, MN: West.

U.S. Department of Justice. 1988a. *Capital Punishment* 1987. Washington, DC: U.S. Department of Justice.

———. 1988b. *Report to the Nation on Crime and Justice,* 2d ed. Washington, DC: Bureau of Justice Statistics.

U.S. Senate Judiciary Committee. 1984. *Deinstitutionalization of Status Offenders, Hearing, June 21, 1983.* Washington, DC: U.S. Government Printing Office.

van den Haag, Ernest. 1986. "On Sentencing." In *Punishment and Privilege,* eds. W. Byron Groves and Graeme Newman. Albany, NY: Harrow and Heston.

van den Haag, Ernest, and John P. Conrad. 1983. *The Death Penalty: A Debate.* New York: Plenum.

Varley, W. H. 1984. "Behavior Modification Approaches to the Aggressive Adolescent." In *The Aggressive Adolescent: Clinical Perspectives,* ed. C. R. Keith. New York: Free Press.

Vito, Gennaro, and Deborah G. Wilson. 1985. *The American Juvenile Justice System.* Beverly Hills: Sage.

Vito, Gennaro, F., and Thomas J. Keil. 1988. "Capital Sentencing in Kentucky: An Analysis of the Factors Influencing Decision-making in the Post-*Gregg* Period." *Journal of Criminal Law and Criminology* 79:483–503.

Vollmann, John J., Jr. 1987. "Neutering Homicidal Recidivists in Jurisdictions without Capital Punishment." Paper presented at the American Society of Criminology meetings, November. Montreal, CAN.

Wallace, Donald H. 1989. "Bloodbath and Brutalization: Public Opinion and the Death Penalty." *Journal of Crime and Justice* 12:51–77.

Warr, Mark, and Mark Stafford. 1984. "Public Goals of Punishment and Support for the Death Penalty." *Journal of Research in Crime and Delinquency* 21:95–111.

Watkins, John C., Jr. 1987. "The Convolution of Ideology: American Juvenile Justice from a Critical Legal Studies Perspective." Paper presented at the American Society of Criminology meetings, November, Montreal, CAN.

Weichman, Dennis, and Jerry Kendall. 1987. "A Longitudinal Analysis of the Death Penalty." *Justice Professional* 2:100–109.

Weisheit, Ralph A., and Diane M. Alexander. 1988. "Juvenile Justice Philosophy and the Demise of *Parens Patriae.*" *Federal Probation* 52(4):56–63.

Whitehead, John T., and Steven P. Lab. 1990. *Juvenile Justice: An Introduction.* Cincinnati, OH: Anderson.

Wilson, William. 1983. "Juvenile Offenders and the Electric Chair: Cruel and Unusual Punishment or Form of Discipline for the Hopelessly Delinquent?" *University of Florida Law Review* 35:344–74.

Youth Policy and Law Center, Inc. 1984. *Violent Delinquents: A Wisconsin Study.* Madison, WI: Youth Policy and Law Center.

Zaslaw, Jay G. 1989. "Stop Assaultive Children—Project SAC Offers Hope for Violent Juveniles." *Corrections Today* 51:48–50.

Zimring, Franklin, and Gordon Hawkins. 1986. *Capital Punishment and the American Agenda.* Cambridge, UK: Cambridge University Press.

CASES CITED

Baldwin v. New York, 399 U.S. 66 (1970)

Breed v. Jones, 421 U.S. 519 (1975)

Davis v. Alaska, 415 U.S. 308 (1974)

Eddings v. *Oklahoma*, 102 S.Ct. 869 (1982)

Furman v. Georgia, 408 U.S. 238 (1972)

Gideon v. Wainwright, 372 U.S. 335 (1963)

Gregg v. Georgia, 428 U.S. 153 (1976)

Inmates v. Affleck, 346 F. Supp. 1354 (D.R.I. 1972)

In re Gault, 387 U.S. 1 (1967)

In re Winship, 397 U.S. 358 (1970)

Kent v. U.S., 383 U.S. 541 (1966)

McKeiver v. Pennsylvania, 403 U.S. 528 (1971)

Miranda v. Arizona, 384 U.S. 436 (1966)

Morales v. Turman, 562, F.2d 993 (5th Cir. 1977)
People v. Portland, 423 N.Y.S. 2d 999 (Crim. Ct. 1979)
People v. Thorpe, 641 P. 2d 935 (Colo. 1982)
Schall v. Martin, 104 S.Ct. 2403 (1984)
Stanford v. Kentucky, 109 S.Ct. 2969 (1989)
State v. Bernard, 401 A. 2d 448 (R.I. 1979)
Thompson v. Oklahoma, 108 S.Ct. 2687 (1988)
Wilkins v. Missouri, 109 S.Ct. 2969 (1989)
United States v. Hoo, 825 F.2d 667 (1987)
United States v. Salerno, 107 S.Ct. 2095 (1987)

Name Index

Subject Index

ABOUT THE AUTHORS

DEAN J. CHAMPION is Professor of Criminal Justice at California State University, Long Beach. He received his Ph.D. from Purdue University in 1965. His interests include the plea bargaining process, judicial discretion in sentencing decision-making, and the juvenile justice process. His books include *Criminal Justice in the United States, Probation and Parole in the United States, Corrections in the United States: A Contemporary Perspective, Felony Probation* (Praeger), and an edited work, *The U.S. Sentencing Guidelines* (Praeger). Forthcoming works include *Methods and Statistics for Criminal Justice and Criminology* and *The Juvenile Justice System*. Some of his articles have appeared in *Crime and Delinquency, American Journal of Criminal Justice, Crime and Justice, Federal Probation, Journal of Criminal Justice, The Prosecutor, Journal of Contemporary Criminal Justice*, and *Justice Professional*.

G. LARRY MAYS is Professor of Criminal Justice at New Mexico State University. He served as a police officer in Knoxville, Tennessee and received his Ph.D. in political science from the University of Tennessee. His teaching and research interests include criminal justice policy development, implementation, and evaluation, especially in the areas of juvenile justice and the judicial process. His books include *Juvenile Delinquency and Juvenile Justice*, coauthored with Joseph W. Rogers and *American Jails: Public Policy Issues*, coedited with Joel A. Thompson. He has articles in *Journal of Criminal Justice, American Journal of Criminal Justice, Justice Quarterly, Judicature, Justice System Journal, Criminal Justice Policy Review, Criminal Justice Review*, and *Policy Studies Review*.